D0757835

Action Modality
Couples Therapy

Action Modality Couples Therapy:
Using Psychodramatic Techniques in Helping Troubled Relationships

Joyce Ann Hayden-Seman, Ph.D.

JASON ARONSON INC.
Northvale, New Jersey
London

This book was set in 11 pt. Fairfield Light by Alabama Book Composition of Deatsville, Alabama.

Library of Congress Cataloging-in-Publication Data

Hayden-Seman, Joyce Ann.
    Action modality couples therapy : using psychodramatic techniques
in helping troubled relationships / Joyce Ann Hayden-Seman.
        p.   cm.
    Includes bibliographical references and index.
    ISBN 0–7657–0064–6 (alk. paper)
    1. Marital psychotherapy. 2. Psychodrama. I. Title.
RC488.5.H386 1998
616.89'156—dc21   96-53646

Printed in the United States of America on acid-free paper. For information and catalog write to Jason Aronson Inc., 230 Livingston Street, Northvale, New Jersey 07647-1726. Or visit our website: http://www.aronson.com

To my mother, Anna Kostic-Seman,
and my sons,
John R. Hayden and Drew D. Hayden

Contents

Preface

$\mathcal{T}$his book is an introduction to the application of Action Modality Psychotherapy (AMP) as a method for treating couples. I began with a question: Can action psychotherapy be applied to couples psychotherapy? Since I found no research or study actually using action psychotherapy with couples, I turned to the early 1930s work of J. L. Moreno to place this exploration in the context of relevant writings in psychology, psychotherapy, and philosophy.

Various cases were employed to explicate the theory of AMP for application to couples psychotherapy. A couple's sociometric analysis, including role diagrams and social atoms completed over the course of treatment, is presented in this text. The clinician's evaluation, including session dialogue, therapist's thoughts during sessions, and reflective analysis are contained. The sociometric role analysis and therapeutic dramatic process of Action Modality Psychotherapy presented in this text provide a unique effective means of treatment with couples.

Acknowledgments

The groundbreaking research for this book was the first of its kind. I am deeply indebted to many individuals who provided me with the encouragement and assistance I needed to see this project to completion. My work during my study and development of AMP was reviewed often by two experts in the field, Robert Siroka, Ph.D., Executive Director of the Institute for Consultations, New York, N.Y., and Albert E. Frech, Ph.D., Director of Counseling at Ramapo College of New Jersey. Siroka (1992) suggested the three-part segmentation of the sessions and supervised the expansion of the method. Frech directed the couples psychotherapy sessions video assessment tools. In an effort to distinguish my own countertransferential issues related to coupling I consulted weekly with Jacqueline Siroka, C.S.W., Clinical Director of the Institute for Consultations, New York, N.Y. Along with the above individuals I would especially like to thank:

Richard Stuart for suggesting and also providing me with a scale to review my clinical work;

Nancy Razza, Lawrence Washington, Leo Murillo, Dror Nir, and Sam Goff, clinical reviewers who reviewed and rated the videotaped couples psychotherapy sessions;

John Cook, for editing the couples psychotherapy sessions;

Angela Kohler, for her endless hours of word processing;

Zerka Moreno (Moreno's wife and co-author) for her services as consultant, and for timeless support;

Gail Ross Edwards, for her support, editing, and friendship;

William McKelvie, for his knowledge and expertise;

Jean Griffin, for her knowledge, supervision, and guidance;

and the couples who generously, courageously, and confidently offered me the opportunity to serve them and develop a method of helping others in the future.

1

⚬

Introduction

$\mathcal{A}$s a mental health professional, I am deeply concerned about the issues clinicians face today when working with troubled couples. By the time a couple reaches the psychotherapist's office, many dysfunctional patterns, such as acting out behavior by a child, physical or verbal abuse, alcoholism, or an extramarital affair by one of the partners, have already emerged. Most of these patterns have been brought about by changes in personal values, lifestyle, gender, roles, pressures of dual careers, or the stresses related to having a reconstituted family. Internal or external role conflicts, role confusion, and role fatigue are particularly strong factors in the development of dysfunctional behaviors by one or both partners.

Our society has not been able to lower the marriage dissolution rate. The need for help with relationship problems is indicated by the rate of divorce, which has remained fairly steady since the 1980s: half of all marriages in the United States today and over a third in England will end in divorce rather than death (Stone 1990). The majority of these divorces occur within the first three years of marriage, and four out of five of these individuals ultimately remarry.

With a divorce rate of 50 percent (National Center for Health Statistics 1986), it appears that some professional intervention in the area of relationship enhancement is needed. Couples want to be successful in their relationships, however, they do not know how to develop effective means of relating and communicating. To develop and maintain an effective relationship requires defining of oneself as separate from a significant other (Karpel 1980) and knowing effective methods of disclosing the self. This includes a commitment to the relationship and knowledge of effective communication (Sager 1976a), such as conflict resolution, requesting and giving information, and listening and deciphering feedback (Weakland et al. 1974).

Action Modality Psychotherapy (AMP), through an exchange of feedback, can enhance partnerships by offering both mates the opportunity to uncover unconscious fears or beliefs and to express the blocks to their growth (intrapersonally and interpersonally), as well as to encourage new in-depth skills of relating. AMP is a cognitive method that can be used by clinicians from various schools of thought, forming part of a treasure of tools available to them when working with couples.

This book addresses the treatment issues of couples by examining the patterns and factors that they encounter in their attempts to find and/or maintain an intimate partnership. In my investigation and development of this method, since I found no procedure of its kind in the literature, I began to initiate, develop, and employ a practical, unique means of couples psychotherapy using action to cut through the hidden and deceptive styles of coping. The term I use for the application of this process of treating couples, Action Modality Psychotherapy (AMP), refers to a means of helping couples enhance their role repertoire, and thereby increase and maintain a desirable intimate relationship. By using this method, partially or in its complete form, the therapist assists partners in finding role relief (a change of role to alleviate burnout), and addresses situations that develop due to the frustrations of role expansion or role contraction. AMP is a spontaneous and creative form of psychotherapy that enables couples to reexperience and recreate their life situations, dreams, and memories. Through AMP, couples can gain insight and develop empathy for their partners as well as new effective approaches of relating. This book presents several vignettes of the treatment procedure and an in-depth application of the use of AMP with a couple.

Most individuals enter marriage with no previous education or training in effective methods of marital development or communication, believing that the institution of marriage in itself has an inherent capacity to produce effortless fulfillment. Our society's belief in the oneness of man and woman in a relationship, united at all times, creates, as Moreno (1939) points out, a continual search "for the other half of the relationship" (p. 114). Each person, because he or she loves and desires to please his or her mate, often attributes the partner with supernatural powers and responsibility for the other's happiness. The understanding that a critical requirement for a good relationship is the development and maintenance of oneself comes as a shock; most people seek to change their partner, not themselves.

Couples need to learn how to preserve the spontaneity of their first meeting and, thereby, continually replenish their relationship with the essence of their unique *tele* or chemistry. A complimentary role repertoire that enhances their relationship's spontaneity and creativity must be functioning. Tactics each partner learned from his or her parents' marriage or from their parental relationships need to be transformed into the couple's politics of love, with each partner taking pressure off the relationship and giving as freely as possible. According to Moreno (1946), marriage has the "stigma of the law and may develop inertia through repetition" (p. 120). Individuals, therefore, need to relinquish nonproductive efforts to change their partners and become self-focused, moving towards change and balance in the relationship to avoid a narrowing of perspective toward their mate.

The trouble with first marriages, noted Linton (1936), is that "most people don't like themselves and look to the other because they don't have the courage to do anything about it" (p. 490), while second marriages are characterized by sweat, with couples tending to work harder at making the relationship successful (Stuart and Stuart 1985). Variables that have an impact on marital stability include the ages of the partners, their level of education and income (Norton and Glick 1979). The main reason for the marriage, whether it is a first or second marriage, appears to be the same—love (Rollin and Feldman 1973). Most remarriages occur within nine years, and a very early remarriage is often a sign of autonomy avoidance, as it is with adolescent marriages.

The idea of an individual's need for homeostasis became pronounced in the late nineteenth century, during the birth of psychoanalysis. This was when Freud's biological and reductionistic theories of the unconscious were in vogue; his psychoanalytic work *The Interpretation of Dreams* (Freud 1900) was widely acclaimed by the psychiatric profession. Unswayed by this revolutionary movement, J. L. Moreno, a younger revolutionary psychiatrist practicing in Vienna at the same time, disagreed with Freud's theories, claiming that the conscious, not the unconscious, was the area of the psyche to be focused upon in treatment. He encouraged a "here and now" approach. Moreno claimed that he gave his patients the courage to dream again, in contrast to Freud's focus on the exploration of the unconscious through dream analysis. Later, after his move to the United States from Vienna in 1946, he said, "I teach the people to play God through psychodrama" (p. 6). In his writings during that time Moreno referred to his psychiatric treatment approach as *psychodrama*, the Greek translation for "soul in action." Because of his somewhat rebellious nature he was not recognized by his colleagues and continues to go unrecognized despite his many contributions to the study of psychology (Hollander 1983).

Moreno (1966) was drawn to exploring and assessing the relationship between others: how certain people exchange an energy that encourages each individual and the relationship to flourish with an aliveness and spontaneity. When individuals lost their "s" (spontaneity or life force) he discovered they experienced anxiety or separation. He developed psychodrama, which he claimed released the blockages of "s."

Early on, Moreno explored measurements of an individual's spontaneity. He found that by measuring the spontaneity between individuals he could further explore the faulty choice patterns (role selections) that developed which sapped their spontaneity. This exploration of chemistry patterns between individuals he referred to as *sociometry*. Sociometry, the basic principal of his philosophy, who a person chooses and what they choose them for, examines the development and use of spontaneity. His development of psychodrama (1953) was based on a philosophy of sociometry that uses descriptive methods to explain and account for interpersonal relations, as well as the degree of acceptance and rejection of others in their specific roles. This book uses the term AMP rather than the term psychodrama, because the latter concept relates to Moreno's work primarily with groups.

For our purposes, the term *couple* in this book is defined as an interpersonal relationship whose fundamental purpose is mutual care, responsibility, knowledge, and respect aimed towards sustaining mutual gratification and love. Couples from this point of view are intimates who have an interpersonal connection and want the best for the self and the other. As Fromm (1956) said, "The desire for interpersonal fusion is the most powerful striving of man" (p. 18).

EFFECTS OF STRESS ON COUPLES

Under stress, partners experience their fusion severed and become outwardly focused. It becomes easier under stress for individuals to focus on their significant other rather than remain inner-focused; to try to change their partners rather than themselves. When stress is high, and remains high for any length of time, the anxiety, due to job loss, a death in the family, birth of a child, an illness, or some crisis, puts the core of oneself out of balance (Lerner 1989). These additional stressors create an overload for the individual's usual coping skills. When this occurs his or her spontaneity/creativity, or telic connection, as Moreno described it (1966), has no channel, no outlet; energy becomes trapped, contained, and turns into anxiety. When anxious, some individuals overfunction. They assume responsibility for others or for all tasks. Driven by their feelings, they attempt to manage their anxiety, reacting and acting without thinking. Keeping their anxiety down becomes the priority. Anxiety fuels their interactions. A long-past experience, often an unresolved issue from their family of origin, becomes the underlying impetus of their dilemma. In contrast, another group of individuals when anxious or stressed turns their energy into apathy, lethargy, or immobility. In order to contain their anxiety they freeze over and act indifferent or passive. The contrast in style frequently attracts individuals who function in opposite styles (Moreno 1977). The difference, although considered an attraction at first, later turns into frustration or alienation.

Married people tend to rate themselves and experience themselves as happy more than single people do; married men rate themselves highest in the happiness category (LeFrancois 1984). It is no wonder, therefore, that fewer than 5 percent of Americans never marry.

A stressed-out couple, in which each mate expresses anxiety in one of the two ways described, often enters therapy when anxiety overloads their relationship with one of three problems: marital fighting, a problem with a child, or some related issue like sexual incompatibility or infidelity (Lerner 1989). These problems seem insurmountable to the partners because the relationship under this type of stress polarizes the couple into damaging interactional styles. A neurosis exists (Moreno 1946), "as long as a controversial flow of emotions between the two persons exist" (p. 236). The couple interested in changing the disruptive interaction seeks couples therapy.

People in search of more fulfilling relationships are turning to couples therapists for assistance in resolving their partnership conflicts. Thus, couples therapy over the last decade has evolved into one of the most significant psychotherapeutic interventions in the mental health field (Gurman 1978). Contemporary couples therapy, however, did not begin with the advancement of a new theory of practice by a single founder, as did psychoanalysis. Rather, it emerged rapidly, as various practitioners and schools of thought responded to the growing needs of couples.

AMP, however, has advanced from theory to practice. Through an exchange of feedback, AMP enhances partnerships by offering each mate the opportunity to uncover unconscious ideas, beliefs, or experiences that block his or her growth (intrapersonally and interpersonally), and encourages the development of new skills of relating. Clinicians using various modalities of practice may find valuable techniques they can creatively use when working with couples.

The vignettes throughout the text and the case presentation that follows (see Chapter 6) serve as an explication of the theory of AMP offer a unique contribution to the fields of psychology and couples counseling.

Gibran (1927) describes his idea of marriage in *The Prophet*.

> And what of marriage? Let there be spaces in your togetherness and let the winds of the heavens dance between you; love one another but make not a bond of love; let it rather be a moving sea between the shores of your soul; fill each other up but drink not from one cup; give one another of your bread, but eat not from the same loaf. Sing and dance together and be joyous, but let each one of you be alone; give your hearts, but not in each other's keeping. [p. 16]

In my work as a couples therapist, I use Gibran's words as a guide in helping partners balance self with other.

2

჻

The Importance of Training for Couples Therapists

NEED FOR COUPLES THERAPY GROWS

Although television, movies, and popular music continue to emphasize the drama of relationships in conflict—love found, love lost—people still pursue lasting, fulfilling relationships. It is difficult to calculate how many lasting relationships there are or the number that are in a state of disruption or dissolution because real statistics on relationship dissolution are only reported when the dissolution is finalized in court. Some couples remain separated for years without divorcing, others cohabitate and later break up without ever having married. This leaves us with no true statistics on the termination of relationships.

Cohabitation, in the United States, has increased: one out of twenty-three couples live together without the benefit of clergy (LeFrancois 1984), which offers no termination data. Living together is often preferred over marriage because the legal obligations are different, or because the partners want intimacy and friendship without a long-term commitment, or because marriage must be delayed, or because it offers a trial period. Thus the couples therapist may work with couples who have been married previously or have not chosen marriage as the means of solidifying their relationship. Pain or loss may color these individuals' make-up.

Many people experience loss and pain from ended relationships not visible through statistics. Having a successful relationship is important to most, but not easily achieved by most. The need for assistance from an outside third party continues to grow. Many believe if they do not marry, perhaps live together or just date, they avoid the pain of having a marriage terminate, but the reality of this belief is not visible to the couples therapist, who often assists mates in terminating a relationship that was never consummated in marriage.

MARRIAGE HAS MEANING

Entry into a marriage is the most charged decision of life. Therapists need to be cognizant of how valued and changed a couple's relationship is today. Marriage is no longer a sacrament: it is an economic choice, having different meanings for each sex. The higher the expectations of the marriage, the more difficult the relationship. Both the beginning and end of marriage are the most important and highly charged events in one's lifetime.

How the mates selected each other (how they met), when their problems started (the beginning of the disorder), and the choice patterns they established in their relationship (their sociometry), are important to the couples therapist. These three significant themes are explored below.

THEME 1: SELECTING A MATE

Characteristics of Bonding

The selection process of partners today is characterized by four features: their equality, the emancipation of each mate from their relatives, the individualization of their marriage contract, and the increased emphasis on intimacy (Glick et al. 1987c). The bonding that holds a couple together, although varying in degree from couple to couple, can be delineated into the following categories: care giving and receiving, friendship and partnership, pleasure and sex, decision-making and commitment, and social networking (Grunebaum 1976).

Aspects of Selection

Love is essentially a willingness to commit to another. "Love is possible only if two people communicate with each other from the center of their existence," points out Fromm (1956, p. 86). Marriage in the future, contends Murstein (1974) will be an individual-centered love match between equal-status individuals with greater expectations, especially of sexual fulfillment. Because people now live longer and reside in larger population clusters, they have a greater opportunity to change partners and place more emphasis on leisure activities and self-fulfillment. The selection of mates in this country today rests upon the decision of the individual. We usually choose mates who are of the same race, religion, and socioeconomic background, and show a conscious or unconscious propensity toward choosing a partner who is similar to ourselves. The possibilities for selecting a mate are enormous, for they are chosen for many conscious and unconscious reasons. As Moreno (1975) noted, we don't always choose the person easiest to live with, nor do we always get the person we want, and surely we never get all those we want. Moreover, there is a tendency to choose our idealized image, an image similar to our mother (Adler 1964). The choosing process described by Schulz (1981) includes three basic stages: the stimulus stage (the important physical attraction), the value stage (exploration of each other's attributes), and the role stage (process of satisfying each other's role expectations). The beginning stage usually seems much easier than later stages of partner selection because of the blind spots we experience when we are in love. However, the role expectancies established in the early give-and-take of the relationship form the foundation for all future role exchanges.

Age Influences Marriages Today

A couple's relationship is fulfilled when it satisfies the emotional, psychological, intellectual, and physical needs of the partners (Bowen 1971–72). A rule of thumb for couples to follow is for partners to express any persistent feelings to their mate (Rogers 1975). Suppression of feelings by either partner damages the relationship; "a partnership is a continual process . . . built, rebuilt and refreshed by mutual personal growth" (p. 129).

Glick and colleagues (1987a) state that marriage has a different focus for each age group. Between the ages of 18 and 22, marriage involves a search for a substitute parent; in the mid-twenties marriage involves conforming to some social expectation such as regulating sex, getting away from home, or becoming dependent on a parent substitute. Marriage within the 28-to-34 age group is usually assessed by how it supports one's career expectations. A low point, dissatisfaction with the marriage, usually comes to individuals in their late thirties, after which it starts to ascend again during the forties, when marital happiness and contentment increase. Marriage in the fifties, as of now, has not been studied.

The seventh year of marriage is often considered critical. Idealized expectations have been exhausted, fantasies of alternative mates and singlehood are at best briefly considered.

Intrapersonal Preparation

Intrapersonal preparation for marriage involves three tasks: making oneself ready to take on the role of husband or wife, disengaging oneself from close relationships that compete or interfere with the marital relationship, and accommodating patterns of gratification to the newly formed relationship. Moreno (1969) suggested role testing for couples, a technique whereby future partners could see each other in light of the "various roles which will come into play in their marriage relationship." The following marital roles were considered crucial: "Provider, lover, mother–father, partner, host–hostess, criticizer, worshiper, emotional companion, intellectual companion, homemaker, roommate" (p. 9). The larger, more flexible role repertoire each partner develops, the more spontaneity, creativity, and adaptability each will have for the various situations in the marriage.

Specific tasks in the preparation for marriage include establishing a couple identity, developing a mutually satisfying sexual adjustment, creating an effective system of communication; agreeing upon patterns of relating to relatives, friends, work, and decision making, and planning specifically for the wedding and honeymoon (Duvall 1967) (Rappaport 1964). All these tasks for marriage involve role delineation.

Intimacy also requires role delineation by the couple for their relationship to grow through the intrapersonal and interpersonal spaces and stages of life (Schnarch 1991). For intimacy to expand, validation by the partner is desired and expected, but the bedrock of long-term marital intimacy is self-validation (Schnarch 1991). A well-differentiated person, although attracted and interested in others, does not rely on another for acceptance and approval. These processes involve self-confrontation and disclosure of core aspects of the self in the presence of the partner. Similarly, sexual intimacy, the passionate expression of one's eroticism, uses sexuality as the vehicle for disclosure of aspects of the core self and does not require acceptance or approval.

Differences between Men and Women in Love Relationships

Although more is written about women's experiences and view of love, and women are known to be more preoccupied with love, men are actually more romantic than women. They are more likely to fall in love first and more likely to see love as a primary criterion for marriage. Although men fall in love more easily and value romantic love more than women, they have less of a tendency than women to act euphoric or show emotions, for they are taught early in life to be more restricted in their emotions and feelings (Pollis 1969). Men also have a tendency to be more frightened of love, fearful that it will take away their independence, while women are taught to control their emotions. Women are much more pragmatic and practical. They have a tendency to select mates who have intense feelings for them, and place a higher value on a man's socioeconomic status than men do on the woman's socioeconomic status. Women realistically tend to profit or lose more in romantic relationships; therefore, they have a tendency to idealize their choices. Pollis notes also that women marry the person they love less often than do men. The intensity of their future husband's feelings carries more weight than their own feelings. Men place more interest in their career, while women place emphasis on their mate selection.

THEME 2: THE BEGINNING OF DISORDER

The Drama of Relationships

Our society has not been able to lower the marriage dissolution rate. Marital disorder is a societal problem requiring the couples therapist's continual study and evaluation.

Marital disorders arise most often from poor mate choice (sociometry) and conflicting ideals that become visible (to the trained eye) only in the choice of extramarital affairs or divorce. According to Schulz (1981), there are six important reasons why marriages have been changing and leading to divorce in the United States: the declining influence of religion, the widespread use of birth control and the car, the increasing anti-personalization of our society, the variety of the job market, the increased demand for advanced job training that prolongs the pre-marriage period, and demographic changes. What we now expect from a marital partner and from the union itself has changed in response to these issues.

Most sociologists and psychologists who have studied contemporary married life comment on the discrepancy between what people expect and what is realistically attainable (Moustakas 1972, Norton and Glick 1979, Olsen et al. 1983). Marital partners find it difficult to maintain love blissfully because their expectations are too high. Usually cut off from other family ties today, individuals depend heavily on their spouses for emotional satisfaction instead of on the extended family. The higher the expectations of a marriage, the more difficulty the marriage has in succeeding, especially when partners expect marriage to fulfill not only their personal needs but many social needs as well (Schulz 1981). Partners' discussions of violations of their expectations do not always lead to adjustment, adjustment here defined as bringing into agreement the behavior of one person with the expectations of another, accompanied by a full acceptance of such behavior (Ackerman 1958, 1966, 1982, Adler 1964, Cutler and Dyer 1973). Love is not enough to sustain the relationship's growth. Often, mediation is required.

Differences in Sex's View of Marital Adjustment

According to Cutler and Dyer (1973), women view the childrearing stages of marriage as the most difficult time in their marital life, while men view the marital relationship itself as more challenging than any particular stage of their marriage. Although there has been little research on marital adjustment, men appear to adopt a wait-and-see attitude when relating. Women, on the other hand, tend to speak up if they believe there is a violation of expectations. Men have been found to talk more openly about violations of expectations related to finances, but not so openly about sexual intimacy, while women are challenged more by issues related to time and care of the home (Cutler and Dyer 1973). In reality, intimacy ebbs and flows throughout a relationship based on the evolution of the partnership, each person's individual development, and the broader family system.

World of Fantasy

An unhappy marriage is the result of unmastered childhood developmental tasks by one or both partners. (The use of projection by mates is a very common coping mechanism and occurs when the individual's unacceptable traits and behaviors are mirrored back to his or her partner. Unacceptable behavior or thoughts that an individual has are often disowned by his conscious mind, and an illusion of the thought or behavior suspected in the other person. Role review with a couple can quickly point out the dysfunction and proves the old adage that what we disown in ourselves we see in others.) These individuals are psychologically hungry because of deprived childhoods; they fight against recognizing their needs, and instead project their hunger onto their mates. A "breach between fantasy and reality" is experienced by individuals with a deprived childhood (Moreno 1946, p. 72). Their reaction to separation from an oneness with the universe leaves them in a hungry search. The two worlds that develop for such individuals, a fantasy world and the real outside world, never adapt to each other. In order to maintain their fantasies in the harsh world of reality these individuals develop blind spots very early in life that they maintain at all costs. (The fantasies that are created as children to cope with the harshness of the world perpetuate blindness and self-deception. Couples need to learn to bridge their worlds of fantasy and reality. If either mate spends too much energy in fantasy, the relationship will be one of disillusionment. On the other hand, if either partner spends too much energy in reality, the relationship will be stifled.) As a result the unattainable object, the unresolved oedipal conflict, is substituted for the fantasized mother or father. They spend their time in search of a mate who will be a perfect mother or father; the more unattainable the love object chosen, the more lovable he or she then seems (Strean 1980). As soon as the individual obtains the love object, the object loses its fascination and deep disillusionment sets in. Individuals struggling with this type of disillusionment, for example, often find their home restrictive because they perceive their marital partners as a parental figure.

Fantasies of divorce by married couples, Strean suggests, are merely a universal phenomenological means of escape. These types of fantasized escapes often occur because one of the mates expects his or her spouse to be the embodiment of the archetypal parental figure, one who gives all, knows all, and anticipates all. The desire to escape is an elemental disorder in a relationship that impairs the ability to be intimate.

The Search

Our search for an ideal mate, someone who both resembles our parent and compensates for the repressed role or roles (unconscious images of the opposite sex), encourages us to develop a telic energy (a validation of subjective reality) aimed at completing this act of hunger. During this romantic love process, our telic connection can be reduced to a basic unconscious unifying encounter.

Intimacy

Intimacy is a process of deepening the coaction of a couple's telic relationship. "The coaction, coexperience which an individual learns in his or her primary phase of development follows through in his or her interrelatedness with partners" (Moreno 1946, p. 61). A woman, for example, may withdraw in reaction to her husband's TV watching. Her withdrawal protects her from exploring her vulnerability and need for more attention and intimacy. She experiences her husband's emotional detachment unconsciously as a lack of autonomy—she has too little and he has too much— she then protects herself by criticizing him. These difficulties with intimacy are found in most marital discord, whether it starts with mate selection, the choice process, sociometry (Moreno 1937a, 1940, 1945a), or the dynamics that proceed as the relationship begins to develop.

The ability to see into oneself and to see into the other while maintaining one's own identity is to truly encounter the other (see page 71) and is the key to successful relating. (This stage of role reversal was developed by Moreno in 1915. Each partner first views the world from the eyes of the other and then, enriched by this experience, returns to viewing the situation from a new subjective perspective. A couple must develop the earlier stages of AMP (see Chapter 5) in order to successfully master the ability to encounter each other.)

Enmeshment

Lacking the skills to encounter one another, couples frequently experience *enmeshment*. This phenomenon occurs when one or both mates lose their sense of individuality. They form a corporation with their mate because of their inability to maintain sufficient boundaries. The partner(s) experiencing a loss of boundaries views his or her mate as similar to himself or herself, having the same needs and desires. The very issues that he or she complains about often serve unconsciously as a means of maintaining distance, protection, and separation from pain. For example, the mate using this means of coping due to issues of loss or abandonment says, "I will do anything for you, just love me in return." Although immature, the statement represents a strong quest for a symbiotic relationship with the partner. A person who verbalizes these limitations may at some point become quite depressed because the image he or she fantasizes is unattainable. Feeling that symbiosis will be attained eventually, incapable of autonomy, this dependent person tries harder and harder and thereby becomes more and more self-sacrificing, not trusting himself or herself (Strean 1980).

Discordant Couples

Depressed, discordant couples have long histories of poor communication (Watzlawick et al. 1967). They are unable to share or articulate enough of what they are experiencing to have their mate understand or truly see their point of view.

Many marital conflicts can be better understood, Strean (1980) suggests, through the dynamics of the negative Oedipus conflict concept developed by Freud (1905), which is frequently enacted and exaggerated during the teen years and later manifests itself fully in a battle of the sexes. The oedipal conflict results from the desire of an individual to claim the parent of the opposite sex. The inverted oedipal conflict is also prominent in the marital state, where the dynamics of conflicted interpersonal relationships stand out. Instead of the child or the adult with unresolved strivings angrily proclaiming, "I want my mother (or father)," or "I must destroy my father (or mother)," the child converts his or her anger into an internal voice, "You are a bad person if you have incestuous or murderous thoughts; stop them now" (Strean 1980). Thus, sexual feelings related to one's mate are denied or subverted. Moreno (1947, 1969) referred to this phenomenon as a blockage of spontaneity. Examining a couple's telic connection, their chemistry, and their consequent role relationships points out the blocks in the partners' spontaneity with each other. As he noted, "The marriage situation and its consequent roles either bring new satisfactions or new frictions" (p. 344). The telic relationship of roles functioning in a couple's relationship is complex. Individuals can connect successfully in some roles but antagonize each other in other roles.

The greatest killer of marriage, noted Rubin, is lack of personal growth, such as role development (Rubin 1979). Burgess and Locke (1945) identified eight criteria for marital success that have been part of the evaluation of marriage during the past three decades: perseverance, social expectations, personality development, companionship, happiness, satisfaction, adjustment, and integration. Many believe an affair contributes to the lack of success of a marriage; however, it may or may not detract from a couple's growth.

Affairs

Affairs are complex dances played out against the backdrop of a marriage and can make or break a marriage. The meaning is, therefore, hidden within the affair, and is always of importance to the therapist. There are times when a couples therapist has to deal with the presence or aftermath of an affair. According to Lawson's 1988 study, affairs happen earlier in marriage today than they did in the past. She points out that two-thirds of the women and nearly half of the men marrying for the first time have an affair within the first five years of marriage. Brown (1991) notes that conservative statistics show that about 70 percent of all marriages experience an affair at one time or another. These affairs usually occur because of marital dissatisfaction. Women are more likely to feel emotionally dissatisfied in their marriages and turn to another, while men are more likely to feel sexually dissatisfied. The occurrence of premarital sex is correlated with a higher likelihood of an affair during the marriage (Atwater 1982), and younger women married twelve years or less are more likely to have an affair than their husbands. However, after twenty years of marriage the reverse is true—men are more likely to seek an affair (Lawson 1988). Therapists need to be educated about the reasons a married person may have an affair. Any of the following reasons (Brown 1991) can bring about an affair:

a distinction and separation between love and lust

a belief that their needs cannot be met by their mate

married to a stable but boring partner, excitement is sought from another

a belief that they need to hold onto their marriage for financial security and find love with another

growing out of love with the partner, they fear loss of contact with children if marriage ends

an acting out to get partner's attention, to find out if partner truly cares

According to Strean (1980), although adulterous relationships usually have been considered part of the allure of relating, only recently have studies of adulterous relationships been more moralistic than analytical. From an analytical view, an extramarital affair is one way of denying the wish for symbiotic dependence. In addition, Strean notes following his study that there are many styles and stages of infidelity. Three prevalent types of mates who pursue extramarital relations were found to include: a partner who determines that the marriage is seriously frustrating, a partner who experiences the marriage as discontinuous because of geographical separation, and a partner who cannot accept a monogamous commitment.

Alice (1960) found that an affair can have several meanings, such as:

1. I'll get you to pay attention (conflict avoidance).
2. I don't need you anyway; I'll get someone else (intimacy avoidance).
3. I'm running on empty (sexual affair).
4. I can't live with you or without you (empty nest).
5. Help me get out the door (flight).

In exploring extramarital dynamics, Brown (1991) found that adultery is not necessarily covert. She contends that a considerable number of spouses reveal their relationships and their mates cooperate in maintaining a public pretense. There is also the healthy adulterer, claims Murstein (1974), a mate who is undemanding and noncompulsive. He or she does not need the extramarital affair and accepts the affair without suffering from guilt.

Any of the above choices may be conscious or unconscious. When a partner can look at the other's affair as a joint problem, there is a strong possibility the marital relationship will survive and become strengthened. When transgressed partners are able to view the situation as part of their own responsibility, they usually find out that one of the following situations has occurred:

1. They neglected the needs of their partners.
2. They were blind to warning signs in the relationships.
3. They did not care to be involved at the time with their partners emotionally or sexually.
4. They were not interested in being a lover and/or providing security for their partners.

Nonsexual extramarital relationships, despite having a strong platonic style, usually have a hidden sexual component (Strean 1980). Many therapists believe any prolonged extramarital relationship, whether sexual or not, is an escape from the marriage.

How husbands and wives respond when they become aware of an extramarital affair is relevant to the dynamics of their conflict resolution and tend to vary from murderous rage, revenge, suicidal fantasy, to exultation (Strean 1980). Although there are numerous opportunities to find out about the triangle, people usually fight hard to avoid their instinctive feelings that their partner is involved. One of the reasons an extramarital affair can endure for years is because the betrayed spouse unconsciously cooperates. When the betrayed partner finally admits what has happened and tries to figure out what to do, it is important in therapy to explore how he or she unconsciously aided the partner. Convinced that in order to survive they need to possess and feel that they own their marital partner, many mates become involved on one side or the other of the triad. According to Bowlby (1973), the child who is (or feels) abandoned by the mother goes through a series of reactions, from protest to despair to apathy. The abandoned spouse, becoming aware of the affair, behaves in a similar fashion. At first he or she protests, then becomes desperate and cannot sleep or eat, and then returns to the method of coping he or she has always used. The dependent spouse becomes more dependent; the emotionally isolated spouse becomes more emotionally isolated; the sadomasochistic spouse fluctuates between attack and submission. There is no such thing as an innocent victim of an extramarital affair.

The Breakup of Romantic Relationships or Marriage

Although the breakup of relationships is now an important aspect of life, it has not been truly explored (Hill et. al. 1976). Therapists treating couples relationships need to remain informed about either partner's experiences with untimely relationship termination or either partner's haste to act out an untimely termination to their relationship.

Breakups are a more dramatic event for men than for women, notes Hill and colleagues (1979). Although women initiate more breakups than men, they are generally less affected by breakups than men, especially if they initiate them. Men have more difficulty convincing themselves that they are no longer loved and the relationship is over. The ending is usually initiated by the less involved person, though additional research reveals that at times the more involved person may initiate the breakup because the cost of involvement is too great. However, most people want to see themselves as the initiator of a breakup and, in discussion, will often view themselves as the initiator.

When both partners articulate their love, the relationship appears to have a much better chance of surviving, and while absence appears to increase passion in a relationship (if it was there to begin with), it has no effect on passionless relationships. Living together or having active sex also appears unrelated to relationship breakups, although most people weigh the importance of waiting for sex until marriage.

Most people who divorce do so because they have found themselves in a relationship where they feel they cannot be autonomous because their partner is unable to tolerate, or accept, their changes. They usually begin the divorce process by acting on their need to change in one of several ways. Bohannan (1970) delineates these ways into six overlapping styles: emotional, legal, economic, coparental, community and/or psychically. One of these signs will be the visible first sign of a deteriorating marriage.

Bohannan adds that the inability to tolerate change is at the root of all emotional divorces and that reconciliation is always more difficult after the grounds have been established and the legal papers have been written. The co-parenting divorce is the most enduring—couples with young children will struggle with the need to adopt cooperative life styles to manage the next eighteen to twenty years of their active parenting.

Although Bohannan states any one of the six styles may occur and overlap with others, the psychic divorce usually initiates the divorce process in some unconscious way and remains as the last and most difficult phase to complete. Although a partner may initially start the separation process psychically, the completion of that psychic phase remains as part of the underlying process until the completion of the divorce and many times thereafter.

Most of us, to some degree, find ourselves repeating old familial conflicts. Conflicts over money or how to parent become colored with defensive styles of communicating, many of which were learned from our parents' marriage. These faulty, familiar, and familial conflict resolutional styles learned in childhood from observing parents' conflicts are the first chosen when the couple is pressured to resolve a situation. The difficulty arises when a couple is unaware of how these conflicts developed or how to resolve them.

Special rituals and formulas are needed to facilitate the ending of conflicts or even brief encounters in a way that keeps intact the esteem of both parties. For example, it would be useful for couples to create special occasions for discussing and redefining their relationship, a time when they weed out their differences and decide mutually to break up or continue their relationship. Frequently a therapist is needed to mediate and clarify each mate's choices and ideas, and bring the couple either to a mutually agreeable decision or an agreeable process of separation. The therapist moves towards turning the symbiotic partner's view of the mate (projection) back to the self for change.

Many times a couples therapist may find himself or herself in a position of assisting a couple in terminating a relationship. The AMP therapist, acting as the therapeutic agent, passes on to the client educational information to ease the process, including an explanation of sociometry.

THEME 3: THE IMPORTANCE OF SOCIOMETRY IN COUPLES PSYCHOTHERAPY

Little in existing psychotherapy makes use of sociometry (the exploration of choice patterns made by an individual). AMP adopts its concepts in work with couples. Apart from Compernolle (1981), Hollander (1983), Chasin and colleagues (1989), and Moreno's direct work with marital triangles in psychodrama (1946), only a few articles by the South American, Perez Pablo (1975) and two Italian articles, one by Parenti-Antonella and Patriarchi Anaiticia (1987) and the other by Losso Roberto (1977) explore sociometry or psychodrama with couples and none of the latter has been translated into English thus far.

Tele

The chemistry between two individuals is referred to as *tele*, a mutual positive or negative attraction/repulsion (Moreno 1960). Tele is considered the foundation of all human relationships because it provides a person with insight, appreciation, and a feeling for another. Operating on the social, behavioral, and wish level of relationships, tele is responsible for an individual's mutuality or difference of choices. Sociometry, the measurement of this telic phenomenon, is devoted primarily to the undercovering of relationships, the variables that are and are not related to the homogeneity of sociometric choices.

Tele is defined in terms of associations, and varies from one activity to another depending on the criteria of the choice. Every person is positively or negatively related to an infinite number of *soci*, who in turn may be related to that individual positively or negatively. An individual's socius makes up his social radious, his social surroundings. The sociometric aspects of any person, his telic selections, his choice patterns, begins with his socialization as an infant and proceeds through a sociometric progression. The ability of an individual to invest his affection in others is based on his ability in early childhood to develop an emotional repertoire, a composite of various telic connections. Some of the questions that make up an individual's telic radius include: Was the individual as a child wanted by each of his parents? Once born, how was the individual accepted by his family members? Was the individual's progress through childhood supported by each parent? These selection processes make up the positive, negative, or neutral telic positions of an individual's sociometry that follows him through his lifetime.

The choices, positive or negative, of others in an individual's *socius* become defined as social roles. These roles represent the way the individual connects with others and the roles others adopt in response to him, all of which make up a clear-cut sociometric imprint of the choices and attachments he or she effectively makes to objects or persons.

By early adulthood, an individual's values and beliefs, although perhaps subtle, by adulthood have become consistent and strongly influence the people she chooses or rejects from her social surroundings. This underlying network, feelings between self and others, makes up her unique sociometry. This process used by an individual (desirable or undesirable) in constant assessment is the central focus of sociometric investigation, and an essential aspect of mate selection and a couple's relationship, therefore a most valuable tool for the AMP approach.

Sociometry/Choices

The choices people make of a mate and the criteria they use are referred to as their "sociometric selection." Moreno (1953) said that "what gives every sociometrically defined group its momentum is the criterion, the common motive which draws individuals together spontaneously, for a certain end" (p. 300). This is the key to understanding relationships. Why do people make certain choices, and what constitutes these choices? The criteria used for choosing a marital partner are based on familial experiences. These early relationships with caretakers develop ingrained (for the most part unconscious) role choices and expectations.

When does romantic love end and the power struggle begin? When the relationship seems secure, psychological switches are triggered that activate all the latent infantile wishes, abruptly or gradually. The partners stop looking for excuses to be with each other and now spend more time reading, watching television, socializing with friends, or just plain daydreaming; their references for communication become further broken down. Suddenly it isn't enough that a partner be affectionate, clever, attractive, and fun-loving, they also must know how to satisfy a whole hierarchy of expectations, some conscious but many hidden. Most influential are the unconscious expectations. The primary unconscious expectation usually is that their partner win out over a long list of candidates and love them the way their parents never did.

Importance of Style of Choice

The manner in which couples select and choose each other for roles and the flexibility of the process is important to the couples therapist.

A successful marriage cannot withstand two people having a faulty tele. Tele is considered faulty when there is not reciprocal chemistry between the partners. If one partner is choosing a particular mate for sex and excitement and the other is choosing a mate for security, a problem will eventually surface. There must be reciprocity of choices for a partnership to succeed. If the choices are not compatible, one or both partners will at some time in the relationship look elsewhere to have their needs fulfilled. A marital therapist can assess the role choices each of the mates makes and the role choices each chooses to perform and quickly find where the conflicting patterns originate. At that point the therapist can offer the couple the opportunity to review and change their choice patterns in the relationship.

The criteria on which a relationship is based, Yablonsky (1956) suggests, consist of the quality, duration, personal meaning, value, reward, meaninglessness, and external and internal pressures to participate in the relationship.

Moreno (1916) studied the development of marriage by viewing each partner's *social atom*. I have applied this principle in my work and use the atom as an assessment for every couple who enters my office. A social atom is the configuration of all the meaningful people and relationships in one's life. Its pattern develops from relationships we experienced in childhood, our earliest sociometric matrix. The configuration exemplifies the closeness and distance between oneself, family, friends, coworkers, pets, and even deceased relatives. When a couple meets, each has an independent social atom. As the premarital state develops, each partner's social atom begins to overlap the other partner's atom. The positive or negative telic responses, insights, appreciation, and feelings for the actual makeup of the individuals start to take form. Later in the early marital state, the members of both partners' social atoms, having become acquainted, start responding to each other positively and negatively.

The significant implication of the themes of mate selection in relationship disorder and sociometry are carried through in the following chapter on the philosophy of AMP.

3

The Philosophy of Action Modality Psychotherapy

AMP PHILOSOPHY AS ADAPTED FROM MORENO'S PHILOSOPHY

My interest in studying couples relationships drew me to research underlying theories that would offer me a clearer understanding of the dynamics of how partners successfully or unsuccessfully mate. In this pursuit I discovered that Moreno had developed his theories on couples psychotherapy much earlier than other therapists, indeed ahead of his time. This fact laid a foundation for my own work. Moreno's ideas helped explain what I was finding in my work with couples. The concepts he developed began to serve as a springboard for my creative endeavors that led to my development of AMP.

In the 1920s, Moreno developed a theory that was the forerunner of gestalt therapy, marital therapy, encounter group, behavior therapy, and group therapy. Later, in 1956, he emphasized the key element needed for successful living, successful relating, and successful coupling to be the ability to act spontaneously toward the problems of life: "The supreme power ruling the world is spontaneity and creativity" (p. 117). This idea had its roots in

Vienna in the early 1920s when he developed the Theatre of Spontaneity, where he taught actors how to use and develop their own spontaneity.

ACT HUNGER

Moreno (1969) believed that we are inadequately equipped with a warming-up process for meeting our environment. We are born into a state of megalomania in which our matrix of identity is as one with the universe. As the developmental separation process takes place, we become aware of our separateness. In doing so, we develop an "act hunger," a striving to reenact that sense of oneness with the universe that remains with us throughout life. Moreno (1946) referred to this as an "act hunger syndrome," in which "there is a continual striving to separate from the universe of our first three years of life" (p. 65). The hunger to be at one with another that develops during the first three years of development continues throughout an individual's lifetime. Our first warm-up, our first connection with another's spontaneity, our first source of bonding, our first tele relationship (negative or positive), is with our parents or caretakers. This provides the finished product, cultural conserve, defined construct, and interactional pattern that we continually repeat throughout life, affecting, for example, our choice of mate. Our hunger to reconnect to the universe often evokes in us a hunger for oneness with other people, which is not founded in reality. A split between the first and second universe takes place, a split between fantasy and reality. It is important when connecting with another's spontaneity that we learn the difference between what is reality and what is fantasy.

THE IMPORTANCE OF SPONTANEITY

The ingredient missing and needed to ignite creativity and provide nourishment to a couple's relationship is spontaneity. Spontaneity, the ability to use one's resources to meet novel situations with an adequate response, or meet old situations with a unique response, is the motivating force for creating change—the goal of psychotherapy. For men and women to move beyond their present positions, they must act spontaneously toward the problems of life. An individual's locus of spontaneity is equal to his or her readiness for action. At birth, children are born inadequately equipped with a warming-up procedure for meeting physical or social situations. They spend their early lives in a warm-up period in which all the objects or persons around them serve as auxiliary egos (expressions of their own mental or physical states or needs). The therapist becomes the catalyst for the client's spontaneity, developing their readiness for action.

At birth, when an individual's ego differentiates from the universe, the ego finds itself in a struggle with an unfamiliar second universe, and anxiety takes form. The ego discovers its alienation from the world. The more anxious we become, the less spontaneously we behave. The inverse of spontaneity, anxiety, causes irrationality and unpredictability, causing unnatural thinking, provoked by what Moreno (1956) termed *cosmic hunger*, a hunger to maintain oneself at one with the universe. Spontaneity is often feared by individuals because it is confused with irrationality and unpredictability. "Man fears spontaneity until he learns how to train it" (Moreno 1987, p. 342).

NEED FOR SPONTANEITY TRAINING

Spontaneity training is used in the AMP method to revitalize the forces that promote creativity, affect choices, and address the situation at hand. Such a procedure begins with the measuring of each mate's interpersonal relationships. This approach seeks to develop each individual's sociometric consciousness and provide expansive spontaneity training (an awareness of the underlying network of feelings within each individual and his or her significant other, as well as between themselves and others). Several terms are used as substitutes for the word "sociometry" in the field, such as social networking, support systems, networks, interpersonal communicatives, team development, social acceptability studies. Sociometric exploration may take place in action, such as through the use of psychodrama or by graphing sociograms. Much of Moreno's early exploration of couples was done through graphing their sociometric selections.

COUNCONSCIOUS

Tele is the glue of primary human interrelationships (Moreno 1975). It is the *counconscious* interlocking individuals. This counconscious explains the painful dysfunctional coupling patterns found in couples relationships. Individuals often come for treatment because, although they experience success in many areas of their life, they remain frustrated because they have chosen partners with whom they are incompatible. This type of *counconscious interlocking* causes them severe pain. Further exploration in treatment often reveals a counconscious interlocking of a relationship similar to that of an early relationship they had with one of their parents, or a relationship similar to one their parents had. Once the cosmic hunger is exposed, emotional catharsis can be worked through and the dysfunctional interlocking connection modified. This offers the individual improved awareness of his or her perception or attraction and improved options of relating. The cosmic hunger can often be replaced in the individual's sociogram.

THE SOCIOGRAM, A GRAPHIC REPRESENTATION

"Whenever people aggregate, a sociogram occurs," is the most famous sociometric chart in existence (Hollander 1978, p. 1). The social atom was developed by Moreno (1934) to serve as diagram of the telic relationships of an individual. It is a useful form of sociogram adaptable for use with couples.

The Social Atom

A social atom represents the smallest nucleus of individuals in a person's social universe, the nucleus of persons to whom he or she relates. The atom focuses on the emotional, social, or cultural points of attraction, rejection, and indifference. The number of individuals in one's social atom is generally small, and varies depending upon one's spontaneity, creativity, and growth.

Although social atoms change from time to time in their membership, their structure has a certain constancy. Jennings (1943) used sociometric measures to study the consistency of social atoms at the New York Training School for Girls in Hudson and concluded that each girl's social atom maintained a consistent composition that could be used to investigate individual differences in interrelatedness. Patterns of interpersonal relationships maintain the individual's sociostasis or equilibrium. This sociostasis, unconscious dynamics, socio-operation, represents the smallest number of people required by the individual to feel complete and experience a feeling of belonging. As already stated, if the interpersonal needs of an individual are not met, his or her needs unfulfilled, the person may not function normally. For example, relationships in an individual's social atom are so vital that at times one may sacrifice personal values and integrity to maintain a particular relationship.

As we grow older, replacement of lost members in significant roles becomes more difficult. When an individual fulfilling one function in our atom is lost, rarely does another step in to replace that individual. This has been called *social death*, the phenomenon that exemplifies that we die not from within but from without. From childhood on, the network of our social atom teaches us the meaning of death long before it actually occurs. Social atom assessment is an important tool for the therapist in couples therapy. It offers information about the sociostasis of each partner, as well as the sociostasis of their relationship.

When a couple comes into the office, the first AMP assessment tool used is the social atom. This tool offers the AMP clinician a quick effective resource—a concrete visual tool that forms a diagram that the therapist and couple can review together. Each person thereby becomes the therapeutic agent of the other.

The therapist looking to achieve a clearer understanding of each mate's perceived and actual position in the partner's social atom requests each partner to draw a social atom. To do so, the therapist makes the following request: "Take a paper and pencil and draw your social atom by using circles and triangles to represent the males and females in your lifespace. First place yourself on the paper by drawing a circle or triangle to represent yourself and write your name in the figure. Next place the significant others in relationship to you on the paper by drawing a circle or triangle to represent each person in your life who you believe is necessary for you to feel complete at this moment in time. Draw closer to you those persons toward whom you have strong positive or negative feelings. Draw further from you those people that you feel are more distant. Make the circles or triangles larger if the person is important to you. Include pets, as well as anyone who is deceased if you want. Place the person's name in the center of each figure." When completed, the couples therapist asks both mates to take another paper (or to reverse the sheet of paper) and draw their perception of their partner's social atom, following the instructions in the same distinct manner.

Social atoms are used to point out different stages of life. A couple's completed social atoms at different stages of therapy is presented in this manuscript. I have individuals and couples come back with social atom homework. Clients are encouraged to complete diagrams of various points of crisis in their lives. In the later phases of marriage, the couple's conjoined social atoms develop additions that make up their collective sociogram.

People who are successful individually take responsibility for themselves and do not fault others for their discontent. (It is important to realize that blaming comes naturally to humans, including therapists. Mates have to take responsibility for their part in the relationship. Therapists need to point out their responsibilities. Sociograms used in AMP provide an avenue by which the therapist can illuminate each mate's choices and role deliniations.) Differentiation is an inner fortitude that Moustakas (1972) refers to as the inner creative courage to openly and honestly accept the inevitable, existential loneliness of life. Thus, people, although attracted to and relating to each other, are not necessarily dependent on each other's acceptance and approval.

Although many variations of the social atom can be utilized by the couples therapist, each has the same configuration attributes. The cultural atom is another example of a sociogram used in therapy.

The Cultural Atom

This is a graph that represents the focal pattern of role relationships around an individual. Both partners draw the roles in their lives using size for importance and distance for the degree of comfort they experience with the role at the moment. The couple may also be asked to draw their perceptions of their partner's cultural atom, and how they believe their partner views their cultural atom as well. When exploring either the social atom or cultural atom, it is important that the therapist spend time with the couple discussing the relationships discovered and integrate the information revealed, which may take several sessions.

The Importance of Normative Data

The importance of normative data from social atoms as researched by Taylor (1977) and some common findings by clinicians using social atom diagrams were found. One of the most important observations I have found in the use of the AMP is that over 90 percent of individuals have between 5 to 25 people in their social atom. Common descriptives found in my research with couples (and supported by Robert Siroka's clinical experience) include: an overlap in figures or figures drawn inside one another represent individuals from whom the person has not developed a differentiation of independence; figures drawn larger are indicative of persons who have a strong influence on the individual; figures drawn close represent people close in relationship to the individual; a reversal of symbols, such as doodling or outlining of a figure, represents an individual with whom the person is experiencing conflict, anxiety, or some unfinished business; figures placed above the individual in the graph indicate positive/negative or superiority/inferiority feelings, with side to side representing polarity; placement to the right of the individual is indicative of the positive or negative polarity of feelings at their time frame.

Exploring Narrative Data

To explore the narrative data of a couple's social atom once the diagram is completed, the therapist using the AMP procedure leads the couple in sharing their atoms. The therapist begins by explaining how unique each person's atom is, adding that sharing each other's diagram will enable them to have a clearer understanding of each other and their relationships. The therapist then asks both partners to identify the figures in their atoms, and by inquiring at this point the therapist may initiate exploration about the placement of figures in respect to placement of themselves. The procedure may include such questions as: "How do you feel about x (a triangle or circle)? How would you describe your relationship with x? Do you feel closer to x than you do to y? Who is further away?" The inquiry is continued by the therapist; the sizes of figures (circles or triangles) compared to the self are explored by asking, "I see you have drawn x larger/smaller than you drew yourself. Does that have meaning for you?" Each mate's progression through the social atom interview needs to be completed in a similar manner, making sure each partner has received equal attention. The therapist asks each mate about erasures, overlapping figures, reversal of symbols, change of shapes, indications of any conflict or concern, and any unfinished dynamics. Once the partners' social atoms have been shared, a follow-up session is used to explore the perception both mates have of their partner's social atoms, in which the similarity or difference between the perception of their partner's social atom and their partner's actual atom can be addressed (see example pp. 231–246).

The social atom is the most common sociogram used in the AMP approach with the role diagram following in as a close second.

THE SECOND MAJOR SOCIOGRAM:
THE ROLE DIAGRAM

The brief following explication of role theory is considered necessary for an understanding of the use of the AMP role diagramming tool.

Role Theory

An individual's creativity, productivity, and ability to express fulfilling roles with others is dependent on his or her ability to maintain fluid, intimate, mutual relationships with some psychological satisfaction, for example, a positive telic exchange with the person selected as a marital partner.

As noted earlier, a successful relationship is one with positive reciprocal tele. At times, even with this telic connection, a couple can experience network shock, in which blaming replaces understanding. Ellis (1949) points out that most marriages fail because of the couple's inability to cope with anxiety, a lack of spontaneity.

One's role composition forms the foundation of one's personality. This perspective developed by Moreno suggests that the personality exists in interaction with the socious, the environment. Thus the AMP orientation to personality development is not static but an interactional model which, when optimally functioning, is a spontaneous, fluid, homogenous composite. This orientation to AMP couples psychotherapy forms a construct that delineates a couple's problems (role functioning) into a categorical view for the therapist.

Role Conserves

Partners bring specific *role conserves* to their relationship. These role conserves are finished products each mate has taken from his or her life experiences to form his or her personality. These roles include specific attitudes, formed or molded into a conserve of roles developed from experiences with parents, siblings, or past partnerships. These acquired adaptational roles not only affect the sphere of people attracted into an individual's social field of reference but also affects the choice of role(s) created or then recreated from one's role conserve. During times when a couple is experiencing stress an imposing ghost, a role conserved, a role interference from the closet of the psyche of one or both of the mates, appears. Many people find themselves consistently stuck in mating roles that are not viable, repeating typical relationships, not realizing that they are stuck in a cyclical role pattern.

Role development moves from role taking to role playing, and finally to role creating. A role conserve is a composite of roles learned and taken, and as a person performs the roles chosen, he or she begins to embellish them. Incomplete role playing as a child leads to an incomplete conserve of social roles. Insufficient role playing as a child, Moreno (1977) said, leaves an individual with a cultural conserve of roles that remains incomplete or insufficient. As children, we first learn role taking by imitating others. If the role learning process fails somewhere, an individual may become isolated, alienated, or socially manipulative in his or her role expression. This creates challenge for a partner trying to change his or her style of relating. The roles of husband and wife, like any set of related roles, carry a complex pattern of expectations and responses. In a marital relationship, partners develop perceptions about their own and their mate's roles, which then become integrated into their total role repertoire. Whether or not marital partners respond consistently to the expectations of their mates depends on their concepts of the roles, their expectations regarding the roles, and the reciprocal roles they have experienced with their spouses.

Working with a couple in an explication of their role repertoire requires the therapist to address questions such as, "What would you like to do that your problem prevents you from doing? What would you like from your partner that remains unfulfilled?"

The relationship produces its own meeting and merging of role perceptions and expectations with a range of actions. At times a relationship can lose its spontaneity and become flat and unimaginative.

The functioning of a role includes complex behavioral expectations and overt and covert consensual interactive agreement. The dynamics of both the role constellations and its functioning for each partner become the illuminating key the couples therapist searches to concretize, for this enables the therapist to see how the partners take on roles for the benefit of their mates or themselves that create conflicts or inhibitions. For example:

L: [In mid session with B., her spouse] Why can't you be more romantic?

B: [sighing and raising his eyebrows] Oh, here we go again, you're never satisfied.

THERAPIST: I have an idea, L. How about reversing roles and showing B. how he could give you what you need?

L: [shrugging her shoulders in consent] Okay.

THERAPIST: [turning to B.] Would you reverse roles and take the role of L., so she can show us what she needs?

B: [getting up] Sure.

L. AS B.: [reaching across and placing her hand on B. as L.]
Sorry you are upset. Is there anything I can do?
B. AS L.: Thanks for asking.

This brief interchange assisted the couple in changing their routine.

Fixated Roles

Rudiments of proximity with others begins to develop during childhood, the dance of closeness and distance termed the tele factor. This important phenomenon, the telic power, is the positive or negative connecting force that enables relating to occur. As the infant becomes aware that it is not one with the universe (reality), two sets of roles emerge, creating both a social world and a fantasy world. "A positive tele separates itself from a negative tele and a tele for real objects from a tele for imagined objects" (Moreno 1956, p. 147). Roles emerge connecting the infant to persons and objects that he or she imagines outside him- or herself, creating for the infant, and later for the adult, both social roles and psychodramatic roles.

The more a role becomes fixed for an individual, the less spontaneity in the role. People frequently become mired in roles no longer viable to their relationships. When an individual learns to exercise role-playing he or she learns new roles, or learns how to revitalize unused or forgotten roles, and a more spontaneous style of relating to others develops. When a couple's role repertoire does not then expand, an act hunger exists in which either or both mates pursue roles that come from a desire to complete a childhood yearning. For example, Alan discussed later in a session devoted to a discussion of the diagrams that he had an unsatisfying relationship with his father; their relationship was one in which there was negative tele. Alan had continually experienced his father's dissatisfaction with his behavior through physical abuse. He later unconsciously carried the act hunger to repair the negative tele relationship into a mutual bond in adulthood, and chose a sociometric relationship similar to his original familial relationship, with the hope of redoing it in a more fulfilling way. Instead he found a mate who was like a child to him, and he took his father's role, again forming a negative telic connection. In this instance, Alan's role hunger (to be his father) needed to be reviewed and changed; the sociometric repetition of the same position that existed in childhood needed revising.

Role Conflicts

When a couple enters the office, they are frequently experiencing a fair-to-severe amount of conflict. Though their conflict may be centered on a variety of issues, the basic problem relates to their role composition—their role complementarities are out of balance. When these roles are in conflict, overtaxed or inhibited, or out of sorts for various reasons, the couple experiences stress. The severity of the stress will depend on the duration and the nature of the role dysfunction.

In order to live up to the societal standards of marriage, individuals often resign themselves to performing certain roles, or forbid themselves the development of new roles, fearing that their partners may not accept or satisfy the new roles, and role inhibition occurs. Marital conflicts are often produced as results of such role structures in a marriage.

If a couple's role repertoire does not expand, as explained above, an act hunger develops. The male partner presented in the later session dialogue review (Chapter 9), Alan, had an unsatisfying relationship with his father, in which their roles were not complementary. He was asked to assume a caretaking role too early, and a negative telic relationship developed with his father. Alan's act hunger for mutual bonding carried over into adulthood, in his choice of a relationship. The role he has adopted needs to be revised. The sociometric repetition of the unrewarding position that existed in his childhood is both dissatisfying and unhealthy.

The role assessment of Alan and his wife Linda can be found in Table 10-1 (see p. 233). It shows how each partner chose a repertoire of roles that represented his or her interpersonal experiences in the marital relationship.

Most of us underestimate the scope of our unconscious mind, as Hendricks and Hendricks (1990) note. Our parents attempt to repress certain thoughts and feelings as a way to have us grow up properly, and use various parenting devices to mold us by a subtle process of invalidation. As parents, they choose not to reward some of our roles as children, or they see problems. Therefore, some roles become repressed and certain false roles are developed as children to maintain the required image. False roles are created to minimize pain, and thereby create a void. The repressed roles that meet with disapproval are denied, and an illusionary perception remains intact.

Role Expectations

The roles of husband and wife, like any set of related roles, carry a complex pattern of expectations and responses. The responses that individuals have to a role taken by their partner develops from their perception of their mate's communication. What they take in from the dialogue includes not only the tone, inflections, and words they heard but their interpretation of the dialogue. This includes a myriad of assumptions from the cognitive and affective mental/emotional files that they developed from their expectations, past experiences, and present stress. Thus the interaction of each mate's role expectations and role performances powerfully affects their relationship.

An individual's perceptions of his or her mate's expectations, and the degree of correspondence between one's role concepts and expectations, have a strong influence on each partner's satisfaction in the relationship. In the relationship between Alan and Linda (discussed earlier and presented in the later transcript), Alan was unwilling to assume the role of caretaker that Linda wanted. He was aware of the role she was requesting and had unwillingly performed it for some time, but then, frustrated, he lacked the ability to negotiate a new role exchange with her. Both Linda and Alan required role training.

Satisfaction in marriage is significantly related to the congruence of a husband's self-concept and that held by his wife (Stuckert 1973). Interestingly enough, two healthy individuals can produce an unhealthy relationship, and two unhealthy people can produce a healthy relationship. The important dimension is their ability to have a complementary role repertoire.

"Many married people lose their partners long before any open breach is manifested" (Moreno 1940, p. 21). This loss of one specific role, or partial loss of a marital role, can exist without further consequences if the roles that brought the partners into the marriage are well adjusted. However, the partial loss may become the wedge that creates the couple's separation or divorce.

Once the deficit of overdeveloped or underdeveloped roles are discovered by the therapist using AMP, work can begin to assist the couple in defining new complimentary roles, and then in training the couple to improve their role functioning.

The Role Diagram

The role diagram is another sociometric procedure used in the AMP process that is adapted from the original presented by the Morenos (Moreno and Moreno 1938). The role diagram is a graphic representation designed to show the role construction of a specific relationship, at a specific time, in a specific space and reality. The process of sharing role diagrams with another requires a high degree of self-disclosure, however, it offers each person the opportunity to encounter another view of the self and then the other. Hale (1981) adds, "These diagrams can be a gauge for the amount of role death sustained and the demands placed upon the person for role taking, role playing, and role creating and the portion of time spent in roles perceived as relevant or irrelevant" (p. 122).

The simplest form of AMP diagram designed for use with couples indicates how each mate feels about the other in specific interactive roles. To implement the role diagram process, the therapist asks each partner to make a list of roles in ascending order, using circles to represent each role and placing the circles in a hierarchical form, with the most prominent role at the bottom of the diagram. The therapist asks the mates to make a hierarchical diagram of roles for each question addressed. For example: List the most performed roles you utilize in your relationship with your partner. List the wished-for roles you wish you performed in the relationship. The therapist then asks both mates to reverse roles with their partner and respond to the same questions, making a perceptual guess about how their mate views their role. The therapist may choose different periods in the history of the relationship, or critical events in the relationship, or a future projection, to get a sense of each partner's set of constructs in role diagram form for assessment and discussion.

Role Disclosure

When working with a couple the therapist asks questions to explore the anxiety that develops when a lack of spontaneity exists and role imbalance occurs between the mates (Ackerman 1958), such as:

1. Are the roles utilized by this couple complementary?
2. Are there roles in conflict?
3. Are there roles being overutilized, causing role burnout?
4. Are there roles inhibited by either mate?

To deconserve a role (Hale 1981), the therapist can stage a scene in which the prescribed behavior occurs and confront the role model.

THE HEALING PROCESS

The healing process, I have found as a therapist, develops through the catharsis experienced in the couple's psychodramas and role training. The AMP concepts developed start when a couple enters the office. Actually, they begin with the warm-up to the couple prior to each meeting, when the therapist reviews the intake orientation forms, the social atoms, the role diagrams, or the previous session's processes, thereby exploring the couple's sociometry. The completed social atoms show the social forces that operate in their worlds. The role diagrams illuminate each partner's role inhibitions and conflicts. Follow-up sessions, in which the diagrams are discussed and highlighted with the couple, encourage further role exploration and role training of desired substitute roles. As the couple develop a more spontaneous and complimentary repertoire, they enrich their relationship.

The AMP role diagramming, as developed, offers significant data for both the therapist and the couple. Viewing diagrams of each partner's perception of their performed roles in the relationship and comparing them to their wished-for roles in the relationship (shown in Chapter 9) points to the specific incongruence that the therapist and couple can address.

PSYCHOLOGICAL SATISFACTION

When looking at the psychological satisfaction of a couple, the therapist using sociometry examines their choice patterns. As humans, we desire to be affiliated. The AMP approach considers an important criterion: which person selected the other and the reciprocity of their choice. The questions for the AMP therapist are: Who chose whom in this relationship? Was it reciprocal? What were the criteria for the choice? Were the criteria reciprocal? Couples therapists must ask themselves what their sociometric connection with the couple is as well. Both partners come to the relationship with their own sociometric imprint, their socio-metric position in their families inscribed early, which affects their choice of a partner. Some aspects of people's sociometry also develops from their parents' or even their grandparents' selection patterns.

Questions for the couples therapist using AMP to ask when working include the questions noted previously, as well as questions related to their parents' mating, such as: What roles did your parents use in their relationship? How were they accepted as a couple by their families? How and why did they chose to have you as a child? All too often there is a sociometric carryover from one generation to another. An individual's sociometry is affected by the parents' response to the child's progress from birth on, as well as the reactions of other family members and the previous generations' selection process. All these selections have an impact on people's sociometry, an impact on their choice of a partner and the roles developed in their relationships. If the individual as a child receives double messages, such as "I love you, but . . . ," the person is more likely to choose a partner with whom he does not have a reciprocal positive tele with, hoping to redo the nonreciprocal telic relationship he had with one of his parents. Besides the assessment of desirability or undesirability between individuals, the perception and aspiration each partner has of the other, as well as each person's actual performance in the situation, is also central to Moreno's work.

Although sociometric attraction and repulsion have underpin-nings for many aspects of living and relating, they form the foundation for the AMP therapist's study. The telic phenomena exemplified in the social atom, and role theory explored in the role diagram, are key elements utilized in the AMP approach with couples.

4

෨

Modes of Couples Psychotherapy

MORENO'S INFLUENCE
ON CURRENT THERAPISTS

During the 1970s, couples therapy evolved into one of the most significant psychotherapeutic interventions in the mental health field. Some contributing causes may have been the enormous expense of individual therapy, the length of time needed for classical analysis, and the ever-growing divorce rate.

Couples therapists, like individual therapists, now endorse a myriad of approaches for couples in conflict, possibly because "most therapists are as poorly prepared for marital therapy as most spouses are for marriage" (Prochasker and Prochasker 1978, p. 417). The action modality psychotherapy method developed in my explication is aimed at offering couples therapists an approach that is not necessarily new (Compernolle 1981), but one that has been underdeveloped and underused.

Behavioral, systems, psychoanalytic, psychodynamic, and eclectic styles of couples psychotherapy treatment are the major methods for treating couples. This section will explore how all of these

methods, both recognized and popular, use the early work of
Moreno, at least in part, as a foundation. Although the literature
on couples psychotherapy is bountiful, the choice of literature in
this section is aimed at giving the reader a sense of how various
methods have knowingly or unknowingly applied some form of
Moreno's early work. In the process, we will further explore the
question: Can action modality psychotherapy be useful as a
treatment approach for couples?

Behavioral Approach

For the behaviorist, a successful marriage is one that is reinforcing; marital satisfaction equals success. Implicit in the behavioral
viewpoint is the belief that marital disharmony arises from insufficient reciprocity of positive reinforcement. Paradox, through
tasks such as relabeling or reframing, was used by behaviorists to
approach the problem from a different perspective (Weakland et
al. 1974).

Behavioral therapists rely upon a couple's verbal report of what
is pleasing and displeasing. More than any other group, they have
developed systematic intervention procedures with distinct treatment modules, such as Weiss's (1975) "Love Days," or Stuart's
(1976) "Caring Days," or Arzin and colleagues' (1973) "Reciprocity Awareness Procedures."

The range of potential clients with whom a behavioral marital
therapist can work productively is considered by Sager (1974–76)
to be broader because of the utilization of highly instructive and
educative approaches that may benefit couples who are not psychologically sophisticated or insight-oriented. The BMT (behavioral marital therapy) approach developed by Jacobson and colleagues (1982, 1985) is widely used by behaviorists, and has two
components related to problem solving: behavioral exchange and
behavior communication. In the behavior communication section, for example, each partner is asked to identify, from their
repertoire of behaviors, those things that have a reinforcing im-

pact on his or her mate. The frequency of these behaviors is then increased. "Critical to this phase of treatment is understanding on the part of both partners that observations have relative and multiple viewpoints" (Jacobson and Margolin 1979, p. 236). Homework assignments and later debriefings of these assignments follow in subsequent couple sessions. A focus on listening and repetitive communication skills starts early in treatment and includes paraphrasing and mirroring. Similarly, a structural communications format for reaching specific agreements regarding relationship problems developed by those authors includes teaching couples conflict resolutional skills that include two distinct components: problem definition and problem resolution, which the couple begins to practice within the sessions. The behavioral approach, however, provides no long-term plan of change for the couple, for this method is aimed at treating the symptom, not the problem.

If a couple has a need for insight, or the partners have historical baggage from family of origin issues that hamper the relationship, more than behavioral modification is needed for a long-term effect. AMP, similar to Moreno's work, uses behavioral aspects in its role training phases of treatment in combination with other techniques to offer the couple an opportunity for catharsis, insight, and integration.

Systems Approach

The systems theory approach to marriage treatment represents a middle-ground method that lies midway between the medical model and the behavioral treatment approach (Gurman 1978). This theory also views interactions as the cause of marital conflict, and points out that the genesis of the conflict is not as important as the current organization of the interaction (Watzlawick et al. 1974). Systems theorists believe that a couple's interactional needs have to be changed to a logically higher type of communication. They see the major problematic dimension of communication as a cognitive differentiation between a difficulty and a problem. "The solution process becomes the problem" (p. 31).

Other systems therapists view conflict between partners as the result of attributional deficiencies. This notion is based on the idea of second-order change, which incorporates the belief that if you do something fundamentally different, you will approach the problem in a different manner, changing the conception of the figure/ground.

According to Bowen (1976), a pioneer in the systems theory field, the therapist must devise interventions that will produce the desired effect on the couple's system. The transactions, feelings, and patterns addressed by the therapist using such an approach can be altered by numerous methods, such as: restructuring or reshaping the behavior of the partners' system; observing and confronting current couple transactions, for example, via video (Berger 1978); altering the means and effectiveness of the couple's communications; and prescribing tasks designed to change behavior. For example, the central construct of Bowen's systemic approach is the differentiation of the self from the pull toward fusion in relationships. Differentiation involves distinguishing between the feeling and intellectual processes for each individual, with conflict arising between individuals who are poorly differentiated.

Bowen's (1976) now widely adopted concept of the triangle focuses on a three-person system, suggesting that this "provides a way of reading the automatic, emotional responsiveness so as to control one's own automatic emotional participation in the emotional process" (p. 53).

The concept of triangulation is similar to Minuchin and Fishman's (1981) focus on interplay between the parent and sibling systems, or Framo's (1981) notion of collusion. Minuchin's ideas of structuring and staging dysfunctional systems is similar to Moreno's and AMP's notions of warm-up and enactment. Triangulation brings into the emotional process of the marital dyad a third person (the therapist), who serves as a buffer, scapegoat, or external object for the realignment of the fusion between husband and wife.

Structural and systems approaches to treatment became prominent in family therapy through the work of Minuchin and Bowen, and both became renowned in the field of systems approaches. Their studies and applications resemble the roots of Moreno's work in the 1930s. Moreno's (1937a) interpersonal theory, written in 1937, and his later role theory, serve as a direct component of modern (or current) marital psychotherapy (Hollander 1983).

Strategic Therapy

Strategic therapy, an approach to induce change, was first introduced by Haley (1963). Although not all strategic therapists operate in the same way, many, such as Erickson, Haley, and Selvini, have similar belief systems: the basic notion that therapeutic change comes from and through the interactional process (Stanton 1981). The two approaches, strategic and structural, are at times interfaced, starting with a structural approach, using joining and accommodating, establishing boundaries, and restructuring, and then switching to a predominantly strategic approach when structural techniques are not succeeding. Such techniques as positive interpretation and paradoxical strategies are then employed. Strategic disengagement is also initiated by the therapist when he or she distances him- or herself from the couple at the point of entanglement, making a "declaration of total impotence" (Solomon 1981, p. 433), and thereby returning the power to the couple. Couples often expect or want the therapist to take responsibility for their relationship.

Joining and accommodating is referred to as "doubling" by Moreno and AMP, and strategic disengagement is used as a means of viewing everyone as equal in the session, with each person seen as the therapeutic agent of the other.

Papp (1983), in her stylistic approach to a systems methodology, identified and explored what she considered to be the central theme presented by the couple. She defines the marital relationship as a metaphor "created through guided fantasy, whereby the couple imagines themselves in symbolic form and then pantomimes or uses gestures to concretize their visualization" (p. 26). This usually produces a highly charged emotional issue around which their conflict reoccurs. She refers to the couple's conflicts as a "reciprocal arrangement," and her ideas are similar to Moreno's earlier notion of the warm-up and enactment phases of psychodrama; she points to the necessity for concretization that Moreno's earlier concept of role-taking addresses. Her sense of reciprocity indicates that an intervention is not productive unless it triggers imbalance in the marital system; she does not concern herself with the origin of the reciprocity, but with "the way partners negotiate to maintain it" (p. 26). AMP, similar to Moreno's early theories, gives significance to the concept of reciprocity in its discussion and approach to sociometry, in which the importance of reciprocal choice selections is emphasized.

Systemic approaches, according to Weingarten (1980), are ways of circular thinking about any situation. A clinician in the Bates school may begin by first broadening the couple's opening explanation, then search for irregularities, gain information, bring forth context to patterns. As Watzlawick (1978) stated, the therapist adopts a position of neutrality and acceptance, since "the rule of thumb is to avoid doing more of the same" (p. 151). This is similar again to AMP's notion of warm-up, where the importance of exploring the root of the problem is emphasized.

Psychoanalytical Approach

The psychoanalytic approach developed by Freud and his followers began long before the application of social learning or systems theory. Freudian analysts specifically known for their work in family and marital psychotherapy include Ackerman (1958), Giovacchini (1958), and Mittelman (1948), although there doesn't seem to be any pure form of psychoanalytic treatment for marital disorders. There are, however various theoretical and technical methods developed for couples therapy by psychoanalysts, for example, the object relations of Fairbairn (1954), Dicks's object relations approach to marriage (1967), and the functional adaptation of Ackerman's work (1958, 1966a, 1970). They all believe that the insights gained by one partner affect the later interactions of the couple.

The psychoanalytic approach gives attention to the choice of marital partner and the ensuing satisfaction, and the developmental perspective of conflict in the relationship. The most inclusive perspective on the unconscious factors operating in the partner's choice is termed "need complementarity" (Gurman and Kniskern 1978), which is based on choosing a partner who will meet one's unfulfilled needs. Out of the social psychology notion of attraction came the common phrase, "Birds of a feather flock together." In my work with AMP, partners' choices are considered important and viewed as one of Moreno's sociometric phenomena.

However, psychoanalytic clinicians believe individuals choose partners who have an equivalent level of immaturity, or share similar developmental failures and adopt opposite patterns of organization (Dicks 1967, Napier 1978, Sager 1976a, Skynner 1976). All use a complementarity framework to explore this phenomenon and consider the ongoing dynamics of marriage to be the process, the how and why, in each partner's choice of the other. Dicks calls this a "collusion," while Bowen (1976) describes it as "family projection."

Clinicians using the complementarity framework believe in the unconscious collaboration of the partners, the underestimated scope of the unconscious mind's selection. They believe that the function of the venture for a couple is "to rediscover lost aspects of their primary object relations which they have been split off from" (Dicks 1967). This complementary framework is much like AMP's concept of spontaneity, which holds that a couple tries to continually recapture the spontaneity they had when they first met.

From a psychoanalytic perspective, conflict ensues from repressed unconscious material in such a way that the complementarity that initially appeared as nonambivalent now becomes reattached to an earlier intrapsychic conflict of the individual's needs and wishes, requiring each partner to change his or her role behavior in response to the other's needs at the moment (Dicks 1967). As Yalom (1975) also pointed out, it "is the reconstruction of the past, not simply the excavation of the past, that is crucial" (p. 28).

Solomon and Grunnebaum (1982) used a concurrent psychoanalytic approach, treating both spouses separately but using the same therapist. They suggest that a couple under great stress can find acceptance and emotional support from their concurrent individual therapy. They agree with Franz Alexander (1968) that more harmonious interrelations are gained as the patient learns to relate first to the therapist. This approach bases its interventions on the concept of marital disharmony as a complex symptom embedded in the couple's "social matrix," the conscious and unconscious anticipation of marriage that possesses the unique intrapsychic structure of each individual's values, aspirations, and cultural background.

Following in the form of the psychoanalytic approach, the insight awareness technique of Guerin and colleagues (1987) focused on the need of the marital partners to develop a more differentiated and internally integrated sense of self. Treatment, therefore, deals with conflict over partners' differences and failures of complementarity by interrupting and labeling the collusive process. The therapist's intermediate goal is to assist each partner in getting in touch with significant aspects of his or her mate's character currently hidden from awareness. Five aspects of marital communication that are viewed as important by this group include: openness of verbal communication around toxic issues, the type of verbal communication the couple engages in (information, feeling, and self-disclosure), the character of the verbal communication (critical, laudatory, or affectionate), and the credibility of the verbal communication (each trusting in the other) and the nonverbal communication (facial/body). Those authors contend that the therapist must read and see through these communications, and during therapy sessions make the couple's conflicts explicit. This approach is similar to Moreno's efforts some forty years earlier to have each partner reframe his or her role repertoire and enhance undeveloped roles. AMP also emphasizes a couple's role formations.

Psychodynamic Methods

Therapists who use psychodynamic methods hold the basic assumption that dysfunctional marriages develop from a variety of fears that a couple acts out (Framo 1990). A person can have an unfulfilled act hunger, an unfulfilled need from childhood, that is perpetuated in an attempt to complete a successful bonding or telic relationship that they did not complete as a child. The couple's social context is seen as a two-ply envelope, which includes the couple's lifestyle and the extended family. Any sources of chronic or acute stress are addressed as they affect the couple's behavior and their quality and degree of bonding. "Act hunger is a dynamic process emphasized in the application of AMP" (Moreno 1947).

During the sessions, the therapist learns where boundaries lie and where they must be placed, where fusion should and should not take place. The notion of boundaries as the point at which one partner interacts with another is closely tied to the distinction made between the emotional pursuer and the distancer. "The degree of marital fusion is one of the most important variables in the genesis and course of marital conflicts. Fusion includes both personal boundaries and style. Two roles are used to explain the fusion process: the emotional pursuer and the distancer, the way they move together and their reciprocal emotional functioning" (Guerin et al. 1987, p. 44).

This notion of reading through communications is similar to AMP's emphasis on the importance of the therapist's bond with each partner, with the emphasis on expressing, in the form of doubling, the couple's unstated feelings and thoughts. Learning where the boundaries lie is similar to AMP's concept of finding where the roles are unclear between the mates.

The emotional pursuer, in times of stress, has too fluid a boundary, inviting others into his or her personal space almost at random, spilling anxiety and emotional upset onto anyone in reach. The emotional distancer when under low stress withdraws, and includes few in his or her space. Under high stress, the distancer's personal boundaries burst with an emotional rush of dammed-up thoughts and feelings. One spouse as pursuer and the other as distancer can form a complementary couple unit until stress arises in their relationship. When critical levels of tension and emotional arousal are produced, the same operating styles that provided balance are seen as stimuli for escalating cycles of reaction (Guerin et al. 1987). The function of a third person, the therapist, in a marital triangle is to dilute the tension and create a displaced issue around which the couple can organize their conflict. Triangles are considered very important to psychodynamically oriented therapists. All triangling is seen as a central fact of life, therefore a central focus in marital therapy. How the couple forms a triangle with a third party is considered a central dynamic. The AMP process makes use of near doubling to accomplish the same.

Multigenerational Approach

The multigenerational approach, developed by Kautto and colleagues (1987), uses for treatment both the biological and psychological endowment sources of the spouses. These authors point out the relevance and impact of both situational and developmental stressors, explaining that the clustering of stressors in a couple's daily life can set off a series of interconnected emotional processes in their partnership and in the multigenerational unit as a whole.

The application of AMP emphasizes the notion that marital stress heightens vulnerability, emotional reactivity, and automatic behavior, making it difficult for either partner to think. Reactions and anxiety escalate and spiral until the couple's symptoms cannot confine or organize their anxiety in a compatible manner. Stressed people become needy, and this neediness makes greater demands on their marital partners, especially around such issues as money, sex, parenting, and in-laws. They often revert to behaving as their parents did when they were children.

Paul and Paul (1975) use a transgenerational approach to help couples discover and understand their parents' past as it relates to their current burdens. "What clients need to access," they state, "is not an operative or comprehensive rendering of their family history, but an empathetic connection to their parents' life experience" (p. 85). This is similar to Moreno's earlier notion of "role training." The tendency is to take on roles we have had modeled for us by our earlier caretakers. During my own personal therapy with J. Siroka, we together discovered generational carryovers from each of my parents and grandparents exhibited in my present lifestyle. In my work as a therapist with clients, I too have found that often there is a generational follow-through of specific familial patterns.

Existential/Eclectic Approach

The existential approach, advocated by Abrams and Kaslow (1976), Bowen (1978), and Whitaker (1975) is a process of action and reassessment that shifts approaches by paying attention to the couple's educational and personal background, their specific attributes, and the process the therapy itself takes. A beginning model is chosen, based on diagnostic considerations, that includes an assessment of the couple's learning style and the verbal or nonverbal feedback required by the couple.

Sherman and Friedman (1986) use an eclectic approach. They believe in the cross-fertilization of ideas from different therapies and developed the *Handbook of Structural Techniques in Marriage: Family Therapy*, which includes: fantasy and imagery work, the use of four main projective types (associative, constructive, complementary, and expressive), and the use of recollections, a projective tool invented by Adler (1948, 1953, 1964, 1983).

Similar to all these therapists, I too have chosen to take the foundations of J. L. Moreno's theories. He truly was an unacknowledged forerunner of couples therapy. The method of action psychotherapy developed for treatment of couples, Action Modality Psychotherapy (AMP), comes out of my fifteen years of postgraduate clinical practice.

5

⨏

AMP Adapts Elements of Psychodrama

ACTION AS A METHOD

The success of a varied action treatment method such as AMP springs in large part from its ability to incorporate both a physical and visual approach. Through therapeutic drama the clients turn into actors rather than reporters. Their problems are revealed in action rather than by words alone. As the action unfolds, discrepancies between the verbal presentation and the action representation rise to the foreground. The forerunner of this action method is psychodrama.

PSYCHODRAMA AS A METHOD

Psychodrama in Greek means "the soul in action." The drama of life serves as the vehicle for the therapeutic theater, the psychodrama. Through psychodrama people express their phenomenological world outwardly: they act out situations from their lives in dramatic scenes. Scenes are used to explore a specific time, place, and situation. The situation is told by the protagonist, the teller who serves as the narrator as in Greek tragedy. The narrator in the AMP method adapted from psychodrama is the couple.

PSYCHODRAMA APPLIED
TO ACTION MODALITY PSYCHOTHERAPY

Action Modality Psychotherapy's therapeutic method uses guided dramatic action, based on sociometric findings, to examine psychological, personal, or interpersonal problems. The AMP method enables therapists to gain insight, achieve empathy, and develop new and effective approaches of relating to their clients. The clinician can spontaneously and creatively review and reflect on the use of his or her clinical skills during a psychotherapy session with a client.

APPLICATION OF PSYCHODRAMA
TO COUPLES THERAPY

Through the application of AMP, the creative adapted process of psychodrama, couples become aware of their obstructions, traumas, and communication problems. The weight of old personal problems or inability to cope is transformed. New spontaneous ideas emerge as new ways of behavior that can be reintegrated into compatible roles. As Moreno says, ". . . psychodrama, produces a healing effect—not only in the spectator, but in the producer—actors who produce the drama and at the same time liberate themselves from it" (Moreno 1947, p. 5).

THREE PHASES OF PSYCHODRAMA

The three phases of psychodrama used in the Action Modality Psychotherapy (AMP) process include: the warm-up, the initial phase, when the couple and the therapist propose action; the enactment, when the protagonist (a partner) is brought into the action space and begins role playing; and the sum-up, closure, or postanalysis, when the participants (the other partner and the therapist) discuss their reactions to the performance and their identification with the protagonist. The director-therapist uses this phase to eliminate any tendency to criticize, and assists the protagonist and auxiliary ego (the other mate) in sharing. Sharing may be verbal or nonverbal, visible as a moment of strong emotion. However, it is important that the protagonist never be left with the impression that he or she is alone, even if the sharing is only with the therapist.

Warm-Up Phase

The warm-up phase of Action Modality Psychotherapy (AMP) begins as one of the partners begins to explain his or her situation, revealing the outer layers of his or her ego. At this time, as Toeman (1948) points out, "It is the auxiliary's task . . . to stir up the subject to reach deeper levels of expression by peeling off the outer, socially visible 'I' of the subject and reaching for those experiences and images which a person would reveal when talking . . . alone" (p. 436).

In psychodrama, the warm-up organizes the locus of greatest strength, creates the possibility for change, and locates the central concern (Buchanan 1980). It is in the telling that the sociometry and role choices of the couple begin to emerge.

Enactment Phase

The enactment phase of the psychodrama in couples psychotherapy proceeds as one partner creates his or her experience of a specific scene and the partner assists by playing whoever the protagonist is not portraying. For example, a partner may choose a critical past injury or unmet need that influences his or her goals for the relationship. Because couples find it difficult to truly articulate their goals, the construction of scenes reduces the ambiguity and misunderstanding while illustrating the goals.

The couple is invited by the AMP therapist to move directly from the enactment of one partner's goals to an enactment of a similar painful past experience evoked from presentation of the goal scene. Thus, the first scene becomes the emotional pathway to a past scene. Usually a mate's goal for the future of the relationship is connected to painful experiences that occurred prior to the formation of the couple, often in childhood (Chasin et al. 1989). When enacting the past occurrence the presenting partner plays him- or herself. The roles of cruel, negative, or thoughtless others are played by the therapist. These roles are not given to the partner to avoid the possibility of negative transference. Once the painful scene is enacted and reaches catharsis, the script and cast is altered, using the mate as an auxiliary in the re-formed scene, where he or she takes the role of a protective or healthy replacement person.

Closure Phase

Closure begins as the re-formed scene of the enactment phase comes to a close. If the therapist has played a role in the enactment, he or she becomes a role model for the mate and begins the sharing phase of therapy by demonstrating how to share. The therapist explains that advice giving is discouraged and encourages a process that begins with a description of how the experience of role in the enactment felt, followed by how the role has affected his or her own life. The mate is encouraged to follow the therapist's lead and share from the role he or she assumed in the interaction. Both partners are discouraged from entering discourse at that time by the therapist, who suggests that the next session begin with any leftover feelings and thoughts from the present session. This procedure encourages the partner to let the therapy, through reflection and integration, take effect and seep into the nooks and crannies of the unconscious of both partners. The lifelike model reveals to the therapist the blocks to spontaneity so important in the marital relationship. Hidden roles and invisible relations become visible for expression and regeneration. An active modality, the process has stages that parallel the stages of an infant's development: "the stage of identity (the double); the stage of recognition of the self (the mirror); the stage of the recognition of the other (the auxiliary); and the stage of the reversal (the encounter)" (Moreno 1952, p. 248). These stages of development also serve as techniques for the psychodramatist, known in clinical psychotherapy as the therapist. The therapist or person representing the "other" physically changes place with the client and takes the represented role, including the stance, and repeats what the client has said so that he can hear his own words while in the role of the other.

APPLICATION OF PSYCHODRAMA RUDIMENTS TO AMP

In AMP couples therapy, the therapist establishes a triangle with the couple and performs the function of both an auxiliary ego and a director guiding the action through subtle, nonverbal cues. The techniques used include near doubling, the double, mirror, auxiliary ego, and role reversal techniques explained below.

There are five basic elements used in psychodrama and applied to AMP. The first is the action area, or the space where action takes place, creating access to all that is real, including fantasies. The second is the director. Weiner (1969) saw the director as one who "guides the flow of the drama, suggests role reversal, handles resistance, interprets when necessary, holds the group together if friction arises, lends supports during difficult periods, and guides the drama to conclusion" (p. 255).

Four questions that a director/therapist must ask him- or herself at the start of the action are.

1. What is the central concern and how is it manifesting itself?
2. What is the contract?
3. What is the central theme?
4. What roles are emerging?

Acting as director, the therapist begins in the present and moves to the past (or vice versa), finding a fixed point in the clients' history when important coalitions were formed and consequential adaptation became problematic (Penn 1982). During the contract stage, the therapist's tasks in making the contract operable include understanding and clarifying which difficulties have been cleared out of the way and making an initial hypothesis about the roles in the person's personality that are underdeveloped, conflicted, absent, or inadequate.

The third instrument is the protagonist, the chosen partner. Fourth is the auxiliary ego, the supportive players who portray the protagonist's absentee other, such as a family member, during the enactment. The fifth is the group or the action observers.

Adapting these instruments to the AMP method, the therapist serves as director, the couple or either mate serves as the protagonist, any auxiliary egos are portrayed by the therapist or mate, and the therapist and mate serve as action observers.

The Double

The basic and most utilized technique for the marital therapist using AMP is the *double*. The double assists the therapist in concretizing and externalizing the inner thoughts of the mates, thereby validating their very being, their essence. Speaking in the here and now, first person, and assuming the same body position, the therapist joins in a co-action with the couple.

During doubling the primary task is to "reproduce the same

patterns of activity, feelings, thoughts, and in patterns of verbal communication which the client produces, speaking in the first person, as the inner voice aloud" (Moreno 1952, p. 244). The functions of the double are to voice the unexpressed thoughts and feelings of the partner, assist in establishing the identity of the particular role of the partner, and challenge the actions or behaviors of the partner. "The chief purpose of the double is to pursue the subject, to help and restrain, not to persecute" (Toeman 1948, p. 437).

The double, the major role taken by the AMP couples therapist, is used in a variety of ways to represent the many reflective thoughts and feelings of each partner. This technique assists in deepening and expanding each partner's self-presentation to his or her mate. During the treatment process each partner is trained in how to double him- or herself for their partner. The foundation of the double experience resembles the intuitive feelings between friends or lovers. As the double defines an aspect that his or her partner is either hiding or unaware of, the partner in response can expand their mutual experience. In doubling, the partner sits or stands behind the mate and assumes the same body posture and gestures as his or her partner. Both partners may also be trained to serve as an auxiliary ego for the mate in an enactment, as exemplified in the following vignette.

John and Gloria enter the office. Gloria's head is slanted downward, and she is somewhat subdued. Her energy is turned inward, making no eye contact. They sit down.

JOHN: This is not going to be a good session. Gloria is upset with her mother.

GLORIA: [turning to therapist] Can I please have a tissue?

THERAPIST: [believing the request is Gloria's way of agreeing with John's statement about the situation, handing her the box of tissues and then turning to John] John, could you double Gloria? Stand behind her chair and speak in the first person, expressing Gloria's inner feelings in the here and now.

JOHN: [moving behind Gloria's chair] I'm so mad! How can my own mother tell me I don't know how to love my children.

GLORIA: [responding to John's statement] Yeah, she's never loved me. Where does she get off saying that.

Thus the doubling technique on John's part warmed Gloria up to articulating her feelings. It also let her know that her partner, John, truly understood how she was feeling. Once he concretized Gloria's unexpressed feeling she became open to proceeding with her own dialogue. Doubling can be applied at various points in the intervention.

Phases of Doubling

The first phase of doubling is an intrapsychic coexisting experience, at which point the therapist, or partner acting as an auxiliary, moves into the second phase of doubling, stimulating more information and eliciting more interpersonal information.

A three-phased doubling model suggested by Hudgins and Kiesler (1984) includes first a focus on supportive thoughts and feelings; secondly, an increase in intensity and confrontiveness; and thirdly, the verbalization of the protagonist's nonverbal behaviors.

Near Doubling: Triangle Building with the Couple

Mates often enter in dialogue with the therapist and not each other, or contract rather than expand their communication, thereby developing an oppositional stance with each other. The therapist using the AMP approach establishes a triangle with the couple through near doubling. Speaking in the second person the therapist clarifies and expands what each mate is experiencing, maintaining a pivotal see-saw posture. This externalizes, expands, validates, and balances the energy among the threesome, creating a balanced triangle. Similarly to the double technique, the therapist addresses the inner unspoken feelings of each mate. However, differently than doubling it takes place in the second person. The therapist moves into a near doubling position for each partner and then moves back out to the triangle position, continually threading the loop between the mates. The process is repeated whenever either partner's response to the other is out of balance, inauthentic, or misunderstood. The triangled loop of near doubling by the therapist encourages the desired balance and spontaneity to travel through the partnership.

At the outset of a marital session the AMP therapist using the near doubling technique may begin by saying "How was your week?" as described in the following session.

CINDY: [engaging the therapist using a somewhat frustrated tone] Well, we fought once.

KEN: I thought we just had a dispute, not a fight.

THERAPIST: [in an effort to balance the emerging interchange] Well, you two, that seems to be a somewhat tipsy interchange. Cindy, by making the statement about your perception of the relationship over this week, you served a ball into the therapy court. Then Ken, you responded to the served ball indirectly by offering an opposing view and not clarifying how you felt about Cindy's statement. The communication became confrontational. Let's see if we can clarify the exchange with some near doubling on my part. Cindy, are you saying that you are disappointed that the two of you fought at all?

CINDY: [shaking her head] Yes.

THERAPIST: Ken, are you saying that you feel that Cindy was not looking at how well the two of you get along and instead was critical, which left you feeling criticized?

KEN: Well, yeah.

This form of near doubling clarifies the indirect communication between the couple and sets a balanced footing from which the couple is encouraged to express a clearer, more concrete and direct interchange.

The Mirror

An effective technique, when applied cautiously because of its confrontive nature, is the mirror. "The mirror reflects to the client in action how he or she appears to others" (Stein and Callahan 1982, p. 122). The mirror technique in AMP is applied when one of the mates asks a question about how they appear, as in the following example. Sam and Pat walked into the office, glanced at the therapist, and sat down.

SAM: Boy, has it been a cold week, weatherwise and otherwise.
PAT: [looking at the therapist] Ha ha, he thinks he's funny.
SAM: [raises his voice] Well, there you go again. What's wrong with adding a little humor? It has been a cold, cold week for us. I was just stating the truth. I should keep my mouth shut, then I won't get myself in trouble. What you want is a mute husband. Okay, it was a good week, does that make you happy? How come I'm always the bad guy? [turning to the therapist] I never get it right. What's so wrong with what I said?
THERAPIST: [hearing Sam's confusion and desire for feedback] Let's try something. I would like to see if the mirror technique can answer your question, okay?
SAM: [shrugs and nods in consent]
THERAPIST: [turning to Pat] Are you willing to try to review this situation to help both of you gain some clarity?
PAT: [shrugs and nods in agreement as well]
THERAPIST: [getting up from the chair and turning to Sam] I want you to take my seat and observe while I step into your role. I will run the scene back from the entrance. [turning to

Pat] Let's go back to the doorway and start the scene over. [sitting in Sam's seat in an exaggerated manner] It has been a real cold, cold week, weatherwise and, boy, otherwise. Yeah, it has been a real COLD COLD WEEK—HA, HA, HA!!

PAT: [nods and repeats as earlier] Ha, ha, he thinks that's funny.

THERAPIST: [as Sam] Well, I was just stating the truth, the whole truth, and nothing but the truth. How come I'm always the bad guy? I never [louder] NEVER get it RIGHT! [standing up, moving towards the original seat] Sam, reverse roles with me back to your position so we can continue. [after the change is completed, turning to Sam] Did that position offer you any insight?

SAM: Well, I didn't think I was that angry. I didn't feel angry when I said it, but it sure sounded angry when I heard you saying it. No wonder [turning to Pat] you were offended. I didn't know I was that annoyed.

THERAPIST: Sam, is there anything else you would like to say to Pat?

SAM: [turning to Pat] I'm angry at the cold way you treat me at times. I feel ignored.

THERAPIST: [standing up behind Sam in double position] And I feel helpless and vulnerable.

This mirror technique at the outset of the vignette offered Sam an opportunity to view his behavior and own his angry feelings towards Pat. (The therapist must remain aware of possible counter-transferential issues, that is, issues projected from the therapist's personal life, and review a session's dialogue as described in the later transcriptions on p. 93.)

This powerful combination of sensory and perceptual information offers new meaning to the couple's awareness and communication and reorganizes their experiences.

The Auxiliary

Another technique or later stage of development useful with couples is the *auxiliary* role concept, when the individual can identify with another's role experience. This auxiliary ego procedure is used whenever the AMP therapist wants to add another person or object to the enactment as in the following example. Mary and Harry were halfway through their therapy session when Mary responded to Harry.

> MARY: My father would have a fit if he heard you right now.
> THERAPIST: [turning to Mary] Let's hear what he would have to say. Go over to the pile of extra accessories in the corner and choose one to wear or carry as you take that seat over there and take the role of your father.
> MARY: [went over to the pile of scarves and hats and put on a baseball cap, then returned to the designated chair with her arms folded over her abdomen]
> THERAPIST: Thanks for joining us [extending a handshake]. I don't believe I got your first name?
> MARY: [as her father] Bill, my name's Bill.
> THERAPIST: Now, I know you have been sitting here quietly listening to Mary and Harry. Did you have any reactions you would like to tell them?
> MARY: [as father, Bill] I figured you'd never ask. People have to be invited to visit. I won't just drop in. I know Harry's parents do but I'm not that kind.

This enactment offered Harry a clearer perspective of Mary's father's view of his relationship with his daughter and her new husband. The couple was able to resolve their differences as Harry's empathy for Mary increased. This position can be further represented in the transcript on page 159, where I ask Linda to assume the role of her father.

Role Reversal

Role reversal, another useful technique used in AMP with couples, corresponds to a still later stage of development, when an individual can step into the shoes of another, maintain boundaries, and then return to self. "Role reversal can be effective in expanding the client's role repertoire and facilitating self encounter" (Stein and Callahan 1982, p. 124). This application is used when the therapist asks partners to take the role of the other in order to see themselves from their partner's point of view.

Often feelings and thoughts that a therapist evokes in a couples session can be traced back to early childhood trauma. These traumas usually involve a situation when the individual as a child had to act effectively and suppress his or her emotions in order to survive. It may also represent a time when the individual was unable to find assistance during an early trauma. In constructing a bridge, starting in the present and moving back to the past (or vice versa), the therapist asks questions such as, "What childhood experience is most closely related to the conflict experienced now?"

The most common use of role playing in a couple's session is when the partner is asked to enact the role of another, or a significant parental figure from the mate's past. This offers the therapist the opportunity to place the partner in the helping role. When role reversal takes place in the real social atom context— two partners actually present, as in couples therapy—the chances of adopting genuinely different viewpoints is greater, since the other person is there ready to say "that's not what I think."

The five specific purposes for role reversal are:

Obtaining information
Enhancing a partner's understanding and empathy
Assisting the partners to see themselves through the eyes of the other (developing an awareness of the effects of one's behaviors)

Accelerating the spontaneity of the partners and freeing their thinking

Answering questions about the self that only the individual can answer.

The AMP role reversal technique is used whenever the therapist wants to expand the empathy of a partner as in the following example. Meg and John entered the office and sat down, turning toward the therapist.

MEG: I've tried to explain to Jim how much getting a weekend away without the kids means to me, but he doesn't seem to get it.

THERAPIST: Well, let's have you two reverse roles and have a conversation about the situation. [Jim and Meg exchange seats.]

THERAPIST: Don't forget to take the body posture of the person you represent.

JIM [as Meg]: I need a break, I need to get away. I'm tired, very tired.

MEG [as Jim]: We can't afford it.

JIM [as Meg]: We never have any time together alone.

MEG [as Jim]: Well, we can go out more. We don't need a whole weekend.

THERAPIST: Okay, now reverse roles to your original positions. Jim, how did you feel in Meg's role?

JIM: I was exhausted, and I felt very neglected and unappreciated.

THERAPIST: [turning to Meg] Is that an accurate description of how you feel?

MEG: Yes, I couldn't seem to get him to understand how ignored I feel.

JIM: You're right, I have been neglecting you. I come in at night and the kids get me and that's it until I'm so exhausted I just want to get some sleep. Look, we can get a babysitter and go away on an overnight. Honey, a weekend is too much money right now. Let's arrange a getaway night soon.

MEG: [smiling] Great.

Under certain circumstances, role reversal can sometimes further polarize an entrenched position and thereby defeat the purpose, as in the case transcriptions in Chapter 7 of Linda and Alan. Various attempts to reverse roles are demonstrated in which each partner has not been doubled adequately, therefore the polarization becomes more entrenched. For example, Alan was asked to take the role of the wished-for father Linda never had. She role modeled how she would like her father to be and then Alan took the role and enacted the scene in an incomplete manner, creating greater opposition between the couple. An example of role reversal is also further explored in the transcripts, one of which is represented in the following chapter.

6

⤳

A Couple's Treatment

The clients in this case were a couple who had had previous psychotherapy. Their response to AMP over a period of time was examined to explore its effectiveness as a treatment.

THE CASE EXPLICATION

Alan and Linda

Alan was a very neat, well-dressed, 39-year-old businessman. At the beginning of treatment, he was vice president of a large metropolitan banking firm. However, during the course of their therapy, the bank changed presidents and Alan was terminated with no explanation. Two months later, early in 1992, he joined a consultant loan firm as a corporate loan officer. His 62-year-old upper-middle-class father, a strict orthodox member of the Dutch Reform Church, was also a banker. In fact, both of Alan's parents were highly influential members of their church and attended services twice on Sundays and several times during the week. Alan was the oldest of four children, with two younger brothers and a sister. Physically abused as a child by his father, who was a rigid disciplinarian, Alan had spent some time during his adolescence in a residential treatment center for drugs and alcohol. Since then, he has become a strong advocate of therapy and personal development. He was not close to his siblings, and was punished for his siblings' mischievous escapades and beaten until he said "I'm sorry, Daddy." His hobby was reading mystery novels (several per week). His self-awareness and ability to expand his perception was somewhat heightened, but his affect, that is, his ability to express his emotions, was somewhat blunted. He had a rigid posture and accentuated speech, although he was usually soft-spoken. When confronted with his image, for example, on video, he was surprised at the harshness he presented. He recently had unsuccessfully attempted to give up smoking because of lingering colds and a chronic bronchial problem. This was Alan's second marriage; he had been briefly married for one year in early adulthood.

Alan and Linda had been married for eleven years. After seven years of marriage, Alan had an affair with another woman and left his wife and two children for four months. He had known Sylvia before his marriage to Linda and, indeed, all three had worked at the same bank before Alan and Linda's marriage. Sylvia was separated from her husband and Alan, who was concerned over the separation, started having lunch with her. These lunches then turned into sexual episodes. Linda, sensing Alan's distancing, asked him if he still loved her. After several attempts at denying the situation, Alan revealed his anguish and told Linda that he was leaving because he was in love with Sylvia. Linda begged him not to leave, and said he could come and go as he pleased if only he would stay. But, after two months, Linda said the situation was driving her crazy and asked Alan to leave. Alan moved in with Sylvia and her 4-year-old daughter for four months, but then returned home, saying he missed his family and would try to make the marriage work. Sylvia continued to pursue Alan with phone calls to his office and home. Overwhelmed, Linda and Alan entered couples therapy. They continued therapy for three years and then stopped for no apparent reason. After attending a seminar on addictive relationships at a neighborhood community hospital, they approached me for treatment. Their prior therapist told me in a phone consultation of Alan's disloyalty and suspicious behavior toward Linda while in therapy. Although the therapist had no factual information, she believed Alan was still involved with Sylvia. Both partners told me they believed that their prior therapist blamed Alan for the marital disruption.

Linda had two older brothers. The younger brother was homosexual. She came from a blue-collar family. Linda's mother was a factory assembly worker who had worked nights during Linda's childhood and adolescence. She was also an alcoholic who did not acknowledge her drinking but frequently had been found by Linda sleeping on the floor at night in various rooms of the house. Linda's father, a diabetic, had had his right leg amputated five years previously and wore a prosthesis, which he appeared to have adapted to easily, although he relied on his wife to do much of the heavy work around the house. Linda, herself, had been diagnosed as diabetic at age 13. Although she complained of symptoms, her parents ignored the diagnosis for some time until one day when she finally went into a coma.

Linda had been seen initially for individual therapy a year and a half prior to couples therapy. Before that, she relied on Alan to give her daily insulin injections and deal with her insulin shock episodes, which seemed to occur monthly. These episodes subsided after therapy.

The couple had two children, Moira, 8, and Lee, 5. Moira had enuresis problems for several years and her parents had sought various forms of medical treatment for her. She was currently seeing a psychotherapist at the local mental health clinic. The couple attributed the problem to genetics, since Alan claimed he had enuresis problems during his early childhood. Linda, although initially hostile toward Moira's problem prior to couple's treatment, had been improving in her understanding of the child. However, she tended to favor her son, a very dynamic, verbal, and outgoing child.

To add to their personal problems, the couple had recently been under a great deal of financial stress. Alan's real estate speculations had left them with several high mortgage payments.

PROCEDURES

Videotaping enabled monitoring of the couple's progress. The AMP sessions were videotaped because it was believed that the camera could better capture the visual and auditory dynamics of each session. This helped to determine how to improve the AMP procedure.

Markman, in a preliminary study (1979), assessed the effects of videotaping couple interactions, as do many other clinicians, and noted that video procedures do not seem to affect the therapeutic process. While most living rooms do not have a video camera, most couples completely ignore the presence of the camera as they become involved in the therapy discussion. Markman's work supported my method and contradicted the notion of the camera being an obstacle to "real" interaction.

After receiving written consent, videotaping the couple's psychotherapy sessions began. The verbal portions of the sessions were later transcribed to analyze the interaction between the couple and myself. These transcriptions included:

1. The actual dialogue content in the session between the couple and myself,
2. My own soliloquy (the inner dialogue that was taking place in my mind during the session),
3. A later reflective dialogue by myself of the couple's responses to reviewing the session and my soliloquy.

Two sessions will be presented here: the first will demonstrate how the couple and therapist interacted at the beginning of the therapeutic process; the second comes toward the end of the therapeutic intervention.

Couples repeat behaviors over and over again. The energy level of the love they felt at the beginning of their relationship becomes the energy level of the hate they feel when frustrated. There is an intense repetitiveness as they search for wholeness, believing their partner has the power to provide that wholeness. Couples therapists need to assist couples in working out unfinished business from the past—the couple's "act hunger." Using AMP offers the opportunity to cut through the repetitive behaviors couples had been experiencing in their struggle with intimacy.

This couple, Alan and Linda, also presented in later chapters, provide the perfect example of a couple stuck in old roles. When Alan comes into a session and says, "We are not going to have a good session; Linda is angry at her mother," Linda responds by asking for the box of tissues. She explains to me how her mother told her on the phone, "I don't think Lee feels loved by you, he always needs his security blanket [from earlier childhood] to sleep with." Linda, enraged and very upset, is speechless. Does Alan respond with some validation of her feeling? No. He shrugs and says, "I don't know what that is like . . . she probably didn't mean it the way you are taking it." Does Alan respond to the unloved, invalidated child that Linda was and still is? No. He assumes the overwhelmed, detached father role that he learned from his own father. With my reminder of what Linda's childhood was like, validating and explaining that her mother never took her shopping, never bought her anything new (all her clothes were hand-me-downs), never was home in the evenings because she was out working, and never was there in the morning when Linda went to school (she was sleeping), Alan then warms up to a different role and a different response to Linda. He manages to say, "I too, didn't feel loved by my dad." At that Linda feels more understood, validated, rewarded for her efforts.

A marital partnership that does not offer the marriage spontaneity does not create roles that add life and vigor to the relationship, instead maintains old imposed roles, enacted ways of behaving that come from an old worn-out role conserve that causes isolation, alienation, and social inhibition of the partners.

During one of the repetitious cycles, when we were exploring the intensity of emotions that Alan and Linda were feeling, as therapist I was able to lead them through some form of catharsis. This enabled them to clarify for each other their thoughts and feelings, and although it was a painful procedure they were able to begin improving their communication style, and take a risk toward a more intimate exchange with each other.

At this point, Alan and Linda had been coming for treatment approximately two months. As can be seen from the transcript, the warm-up to this session began with a discussion of Alan's physical pains over the last few months, and my struggle to place Linda in the helping role.

In this session, Alan came in very warmed up. As they spoke they seemed overheated, intense, and out of control. Although I expected them, I was not warmed up to the issues at hand. The weaving of projection, with which each partner was relating, was at first puzzling to me although familiar. I had listened to this pattern of theirs before and helped them through to some resolution, but apparently not completely, because here they were again.

The futility of the situation they were caught in was obvious. Linda, who has a serious diabetic illness that she does not manage well, was looking outward to Alan, whose illnesses, although evident, had none of the serious chronic aspects of her problem. Alan has emotional difficulties and is detached from his feelings. Avoiding focusing on his emotional emptiness, which is a chronic problem, he fixates instead on his many minor, annoying physical symptoms. Both partners are suffering from the same problem: a mind misfocused and an undernourished relationship.

One of the most useful, basic, and important concepts discussed earlier is that of the double, the therapist speaking for the client. Shortly after the sessions began, it dawned upon me that through use of the doubling concept I could exemplify to each partner what they were actually saying, and what they actually meant. At that point doubling was utilized to enable Alan to express his need for some space and time alone.

POSSIBILITIES OF COUNTERTRANSFERENCE

The therapist must also define his or her own sociometric connection with the couple. Any possibilities of countertransference will be headed off at the pass. Better to be aware of the possibilities operating in oneself as the therapist, prior to deeper work, than to have some comment sprout from your mouth. This will be further addressed in a later chapter.

Questions for the therapist to ask him- or herself when working with the couple include:

Does the couple remind me of any other couple in my personal life?

Do either of the partners remind me of anyone in my own life?

What feelings am I having in response to this couple's interaction right now, and when have I had them before?

A BALANCING ACT FOR THE THERAPIST

Jokingly, I attempted early in the session to have the couple reverse roles, hoping to have them acquire some empathy for each other. Of course, in my need to help them clarify the situation, I did this too quickly. As you will notice in the dialogue, Linda had not been doubled enough by me, so she did not feel validated enough to take Alan's role, but I jumped in to reassure her.

After that move the role reversal proceeded well enough until Linda, who has boundary issues, lost the role of her husband, and Alan, who feels his boundaries invaded too easily and too often by Linda, pointed the move out to her. With some prompting she regained her position. Had I not waited for her to prove to him that she could do the role reversal, I would have ended it then. So the role reversal again continued until Alan lost his boundaries and blamed it on his cold. Somatizing is the safety defense zone for this couple. (If I falter it is because of some physical ailment, not because I might be helpless, or in need, or angry.)

After the role reversal it would have been helpful to have each partner review what the other's role was like, what insights were gained, and assist each in deroling. However, the role reversal had warmed Alan up to the issue he had with Linda. This was about her not warming him up to her desire for affection. His recollection of angry thoughts had interrupted his role reversal. Following exploration of these issues in the session, the therapist enabled Alan and Linda to get into a discussion about their frustrations with each other and the physical and emotional aspects of their relationship, and their struggle for intimacy. The following chapter will clarify these therapeutic moments.

7

⌇

Transcript of a
Beginning Session

Session Dialogue

[Alan and Linda come into the office, Alan looking haggard and coughing loudly.]

THERAPIST: Don't tell me you have a cold. [Alan has been ill in one form or another for several months since the therapy process began.]

Therapist Soliloquy

This client keeps somatizing. I don't know what to do. I wonder if I'm clearly making him aware of that, or at least aware that he is having difficulty getting in touch with his emotions. What I need to do is articulate his feelings for him, double them. I feel like I've been doing that. In fact, I guess at some level I'm getting tired of continually trying to warm him up and seeing no change, like a car with a dead battery.

ALAN: Yes [laughing], that will be our topic for today.

THERAPIST: All right! Do you have the same reaction, Linda?

Hey, Joyce, it sounds like you're angry at him. You're looking at Linda to see if she is on your side and trying to have your feelings validated; you're not really stating what they are. That's not moving toward doubling him, is it?

LINDA: He's going to another doctor. [As she says this, she hands Alan the video release I gave them last week to read over and return this week.] Here, you have to sign it, too.

THERAPIST: [Viewing the signed release that Alan has signed.] Wow, there is definitely a distinction between the two handwritings.

Now there's the issue of Alan's illness, there's Linda's statement to Alan as if he was a little boy saying, "You have to sign this" and now you've added something about the distinction in handwriting. Is that to confuse matters or just to state how overwhelmed you are?

LINDA: Everybody always asks him if he is a doctor with that signature. [Alan shrugs in response to her comment.]

THERAPIST: [responding to Alan's shrug] Isn't this how you started feeling ill last time, with a cold?

Well, I think I'll just go back to the original theme here, which was Alan's difficulty. I could have responded when Linda said everyone thinks he's a doctor by doubling him, but now it is too late. I could have doubled him and said "All these expectations are very overwhelming." I could have done that, but it's past the fact now. I feel so inadequate right now.

ALAN: Yeah, back in June or July. Then it was a chest cold.

THERAPIST: And after that it was . . .

LINDA: [responding before Alan finishes his next coughing spell] It was your ear.

THERAPIST: And then it was . . .

Joyce, I know you're thinking through the chronological aspects of his illness but you are not doubling him. When are you going to double him instead of demanding that he figure out what's going on?

ALAN: Coughing.

THERAPIST: And then it was your teeth.

ALAN: My back.

THERAPIST: Well, at least it's back to your head.

ALAN: Last time it started as a head cold. But I wasn't congested.

THERAPIST: Is your body giving you a message?

Joyce, instead of asking him if his body is giving him a message, double the message you hear.

ALAN: I don't know. It's telling me middle age is here. I'm now actually closer to 40 than 39. It's complaining about 30 years of abuse.

THERAPIST: Well, what about the first 10 years of your life?

Joyce, before you ask this man to go back and understand how he learned to somatize, you need to double him. You are impatient and annoyed apparently. But what are you annoyed about?

ALAN: As a kid I didn't abuse it.

THERAPIST: [recalling the physical abuse Alan sustained as a child from his father] No, your father did.

ALAN: Well, that's true, but as a kid I exercised, I didn't smoke, I ate what my parents told me to.

THERAPIST: You're not smoking, are you?

ALAN: [avoiding the question] It's everything else that is falling apart.

THERAPIST: Everything?

ALAN: Everything! [He begins to cough again.]

THERAPIST: [hearing Linda mutter] Do you have a comment, Linda?

LINDA: He doesn't take good care of himself.

ALAN: She thinks I should take vitamin C.

LINDA: This morning I said to him, "Why don't you take a cold pill or something?" and he said, "I told you this before, I don't take a cold pill unless I feel worse. [louder] I don't want to take it." I said to him, "Look, I don't always agree with Joyce with the vitamin stuff but if you did take some

aspirin and vitamin C and
nothing happened—what's
the big deal?"

ALAN: It isn't a cold, it's just that
my ears and throat are
irritated.

LINDA: [mimicking Alan] The
American Medical Association
says there is no proof that
vitamin C does anything for
colds.

THERAPIST: Are you reversing
roles?

Instead of asking her if she is
reversing roles when she is
mimicking the American Medical
Association, why not double her?
You're not doubling, Joyce. You
need to double her and say, "I'm
irritated with you, Alan, you're
not taking care of yourself and it
makes me feel frustrated and
helpless." You're not doubling,
Joyce!

LINDA: No, we just had this
conversation this morning. He
never listens.

ALAN: I've taken vitamin C
before, and it just doesn't do
anything.

LINDA: Well, the American
Medical Association doesn't
think anything about
chiropractors either, but of
late, you think they're God's
gift to the world.

ALAN: For back problems, despite
all those brochures in his
office, I . . .

LINDA: What did you take the brochures for?

ALAN: Just because I wanted to read them. See what they had to say. If I had an ear infection or a . . .

LINDA: [interrupting Alan] So why did you tell me I should take the children to the chiropractor?

ALAN: I was being facetious.

LINDA: You were not. You were as serious as can be. [turning to the therapist] Here he is sick and he went out and bought beer. He said beer would make his cold feel better.

ALAN: Beer does make me feel better. [turning to the therapist] And we argued about it all weekend.

THERAPIST: What did you argue about?

I think at this point when she mentioned about his going out and buying beer, you needed to again double for her because the purchase of beer probably elicited fear in her since her mother's an alcoholic and drinks beer incessantly.

ALAN: I don't know.

LINDA: We argued only this morning.

ALAN: We argued all weekend.

THERAPIST: Oh, you must be feeling better, or she must think you're feeling better if you are arguing. You haven't

Well, isn't that a nice way for you to get out of this, Joyce? The point is that neither one of them is relating how they're feeling told me you argued all weekend in some time.

ALAN: We argued constantly all weekend.

THERAPIST: It sounds as if you were in battle.

ALAN: The cold was just the topping on the cake.

THERAPIST: Let's hear your side of it.

ALAN: [turning to Linda] What did we argue about?

LINDA: Different things . . . our not going with Arlene and Sam on Sunday . . . whether to cut down the tree in front, and something else.

THERAPIST: That's three days of arguing?

LINDA: I guess it was three days. I think two of them were connected with his being sick all weekend and that

toward the other. You needed to double them, but you're too angry.

I think this would be a perfect opportunity to point out to Alan that he must have an idea of what the argument was about rather than again giving her the opportunity to criticize him, which is what she's been doing for the last ten minutes, and then getting angry at her. When there's arguing, there's something that she wants to say that's not being said or he doesn't want discussed. I just seem to be missing the mark at the moment. I'll figure out what.

prevented us from going out
with our friends. It could have
been a nice day.

THERAPIST: [turning to Alan]
What issues annoyed you?

Joyce, why are you asking Alan
what issues annoyed him, when
you know it's usually because
Linda has not expressed
something hidden that is
annoying her, and therefore she is
being critical?

ALAN: I wasn't annoyed, she was.

THERAPIST: Which one of those
issues that annoyed her,
annoyed you because she got
annoyed?

Boy, is that statement hard to
understand, and irrelevant at this
point. I know you believe that he
is usually able to distinguish the
issues involved in their
arguments. However, by the time
he pulls them out and points
them out to you, she still will not
have been doubled and the
aggression she's hiding behind the
criticism will remain
unexpressed.

ALAN: It didn't seem like anything
specific. She was just
snapping at me all weekend.

THERAPIST: You couldn't get a
handle on exactly what it was?
[hearing Linda muttering]
Linda, what are these
comments you are making in
the background?

ALAN: Yes, I want to hear them,
too.

LINDA: All right, I'm curious to
know why you think we
wouldn't have had a good time

At this point, before Alan
responds to Linda's question
about Sunday afternoon, you

if we went out with the kids on Sunday.

ought to double Linda's anger and frustration and help her expand on how she felt in response to their not going out instead of allowing her to continue questioning. She's using a question to Alan as a means of bypassing her own aggression and her own feelings of frustration and helplessness.

ALAN: Well, that was Sunday afternoon and we had been arguing steadily since Friday night. By then I just didn't feel like going out and having a nice afternoon.

THERAPIST: [doubling Alan] Bad enough I had to be in the house with you, do you think I wanted to go out in public with you like that? Isn't that what you're saying?

ALAN: Yeah, I wanted to be by myself.

LINDA: Well, I feel if you go out with other people, you break your routine and you end up feeling better.

THERAPIST: [turning to Linda] You thought that since you were arguing and arguing, if you went out you could break it. And Alan was saying, "I've been with you, all you do is argue, so I just want to be by myself."

LINDA: Well, I didn't see us as arguing and arguing all weekend.

THERAPIST: Okay, but he did.

LINDA: And that wasn't the only reason I wanted to go out. We never go out over the weekends with our kids lately and I just . . . [shrugging and in tears she stops in mid-sentence]

THERAPIST: I have a hunch, I could be wrong but let me try it out. [turning to Linda] Why don't you tell Alan what's bugging you? Go behind your chair and double yourself.

LINDA: Which part?

THERAPIST: Start from Friday and tell him what's bugging you.

LINDA: I don't remember what started it.

THERAPIST: Listen, Linda, you don't have to pick an instance, just tell him what's bugging you.

LINDA: It always comes back to me.

THERAPIST: [believing Linda is going to go into "why is it that

Joyce, continue to expand on Linda's inner feelings. You can see she is having difficulty in reversing roles and understanding where he is coming from. Help her. Double him at this point, instead of saying "okay." Then double him so that he can expand his feelings and she can get a clearer perception of them.

Well, finally, Joyce, you've gotten hold of what's going on by encouraging Linda to double herself, or at least encouraging her to put herself out there so you can double her once you figure out what's happening.

Well, thank you, Joyce. Now you're at least being direct and offering them some form of direction.

[beginning of enactment] A role reversal suggestion here is

I have to reveal my feelings"] This is a perfect time to reverse roles. [turning to Alan] This is a great way to get rid of your cold. See, you don't have a cold anymore. You're Linda.

a possibility, but may not work because Alan's feelings have not been doubled and certainly Linda's anger has not been doubled, so how can she possibly role reverse? She's not going to be able to double Alan when she hasn't expressed her anger. Yes, this is a ritual Linda goes through when she says to herself "Oh, oh, poor me, I'm always the one who has to bring out my angry feelings." Perhaps you're frustrated with her but then express it that way, say to her, "Linda, I am really frustrated. Here we go again with your usual, 'Oh poor victimized me, why do I have to make the first overture?' You're making the overture because you are the one who is holding in your feelings. Alan may have some feelings that are buried somewhere, but he is not aware of them. He's detached. But you at least are aware of your feelings, so try not to repress them." So let me see if I can help her say them. Double her, Joyce. Oh well, you already said "role reverse," and you can't change the procedure now!

Role Reversal

THERAPIST: So, what's bugging you, Linda?

ALAN: [as Linda] Well, what started it was we were watching television.

THERAPIST: On Friday?

ALAN: [as Linda] No, it wasn't Friday, it was during the week.

THERAPIST: You were watching TV . . . and how did the conversation start?

ALAN: [as Linda] How come you don't give me any kisses any more?

[Linda as Alan doesn't respond verbally and turns away.]

THERAPIST: Ask again, maybe Alan didn't hear you.

ALAN: [as Linda] [louder] How come you don't give me little kisses anymore?

LINDA: [as Alan] [loudly] I don't know if I ever gave you little kisses. Okay, so I don't know if I ever give them, if I ever did or what, but I don't want to talk about it. Okay?

THERAPIST: Can you describe what you're feeling when you say "okay"? Double the role.

ALAN: [as Linda] Oh.

THERAPIST: Go ahead, respond from behind the chair.

Good, you set the scene.

Well, this only indicates that your other hunch was right. Linda cannot reverse roles and be Alan when she has such hostile feelings toward him. However, I guess you are going to try again instead of admitting it was an untimely procedure.

At last, now I think that you are encouraging Alan as Linda to double his wife's angry feelings, and that's helpful because apparently he is able to do that

ALAN: [as Linda] I feel rejected.
THERAPIST: You're feeling
   rejected . . . in what way?
ALAN: [as Linda] Well, I feel like
   I'm unloved.
THERAPIST: [doubling for Alan as
   Linda] You never want me.
   You don't spend any time with
   me.

and at least encourage Linda to
be aware of her feelings, and also
to realize that her husband is, in
fact, aware of them also.

That's an interesting aspect of
doubling. However, these
comments you make about never
being wanted and his never
spending any time with her would
have been a clearer message had
you done it before the roles were
reversed in the double position.

LINDA: [as Alan] Well, that's your
   problem. Whose are your
   feelings? Those aren't my
   feelings.

Well, good, at least now Linda is
in the role as her husband and
seems to have gotten back to
remembering and expressing the
role accurately.

ALAN: [as Linda] You caused it.
LINDA: [as Alan] I can't cause
   what you're feeling.
ALAN: [as Linda] But you can
   help it.
THERAPIST: [doubling for Alan as
   Linda] Where do you think it
   comes from?

Okay, Joyce, you're going to
double Alan's perception as Linda
to help expand it and that may
help Linda gain a clearer
understanding of her feelings.
However, it may get a little
confusing. But her feelings need
to be expanded and validated and
her husband is doing some of it,
so go ahead, do your best!

ALAN: [as Linda] I can't help it!

THERAPIST: [doubling for Alan as Linda] I get tired when you start doing this, you know.

LINDA: [as Alan] Well, talk to Joyce about it.

ALAN: [as Linda] All you do is sit there and watch television. You don't pay any attention to me or the kids.

THERAPIST: [doubling for Alan as Linda] We can't even have a decent argument unless we go to Joyce's. I can't even talk to you.

I think you could have expanded Linda's envy. "The fact that you're able to talk to me with Joyce as a mediator, and every time we're alone at home you feel intimidated or ignore me or go inside and say we'll wait to discuss that when we go to Joyce's." That would have been good doubling, that really needs to be expanded and clarified. You had an opportunity here. Well, I'm sure there will be another one.

LINDA: [as Alan] Because we can't argue. You never want to listen. You just have your point of view and that's it. You're not going to listen. So I'm not going to waste my time arguing about it.

ALAN: [as Linda] No, that's you, not me.

THERAPIST: [Turning to Linda as Alan] He's telling you he believes you got the roles mixed up.

First of all, Joyce, I'm not surprised she got the roles mixed up. You have this Greek chorus doubling her, which has warmed her up to her own feelings, and where can she go with them in his role? Secondly, Alan is correct. The statement she is making is about herself and not about him. She believes it is a statement about him because she is projecting. Therefore, this would be a perfect time to stop the action. Put both of the people back in their roles and expand on this issue instead of continuing. Expand on the issues that they have gotten warmed up to in the role reversal: their feelings of never being listened to and frustration with the time wasted in their circular pattern of arguing.

LINDA: No, that's what he says when . . .

THERAPIST: No, no, stay in the role. You're doing fine.

Joyce, Linda was obviously having difficulty with the role reversal from the beginning. You're giving the woman a harder time than the man, just like you give yourself in mating roles. She needs support, validation, and encouragement and you're just telling her, go ahead and work harder. These are your own personal issues.

LINDA: Oh.

ALAN: [as Linda] You're the one who never listens.

LINDA: [as Alan] You don't even talk to me. You wait for the commercials. What am I supposed to listen about?

ALAN: [as Linda] You're supposed to be attentive to me.

LINDA: [as Alan] What do you mean, I'm supposed to be attentive to you?

ALAN: [as Linda] You know how I feel, about my mother and my relationship with . . .

LINDA: [as Alan] Well, that's something that you have to work out. You can't look to me to work it out for you.

ALAN: [as Linda] But you could help . . . because you're the same way they are.

THERAPIST: What do you mean, the same way?

LINDA: [as Alan] Well, you just think I treat you the same way. You don't pick out the nice things I do for you, you just pick out the things that . . .

ALAN: [as Linda] You don't do any nice things. When was the last time you bought me flowers?

THERAPIST: [doubling for Alan as Linda] Or given me a kiss?

I don't really know if that was necessary. He's doing pretty good by himself. What was your point?

LINDA: [as Alan] I give you a kiss every morning and every night. If you don't want it, I won't give it to you anymore.

THERAPIST: [doubling for Alan as Linda] See, I can't even mention anything anymore, because if I do bring it up, I'll get even less than I'm getting now.

LINDA: [as Alan] But you're not happy with what you have. It's not easy for me to bring this stuff up either, but you have to get it out of me.

THERAPIST: [doubling as Alan for Linda] I always have to get it out of you?

LINDA: [as Alan] If you want something, you have to do it.

ALAN: [as Linda] See, I'm always the one who has to change in order to do something.

THERAPIST: [doubling for Alan as Linda] I'm always the one who has to change, I'm always working on changing myself, and what are you doing? All you're doing is getting sick.

LINDA: [as Alan] Yeah, like I want to be sick. Right!

THERAPIST: [doubling for Alan as Linda] I have to put up with you being sick, besides . . .

LINDA: [as Alan] What do you have to put up with?

ALAN: [as Linda] I have to listen to you sneezing and snorting and blowing your nose. . . . You keep me awake and you won't even take anything so you'll feel better.

LINDA: [as Alan] Because I told you. I told you before and I'm telling you now . . . it doesn't make me feel better! So what am I taking it for? Does it make you feel better?

THERAPIST: [doubling Alan as
Linda] That's right. Because I
feel very helpless with you
lately. You're sick all the time.

LINDA: [as Alan] Well, I didn't
make myself sick. I don't like
it anymore than you do.

THERAPIST: [Alan as Linda] I
don't know about that.

LINDA: [as Alan] Do you think I
enjoy this?

ALAN: [as Linda] Sometimes.

LINDA: [as Alan] Think what you
want. I'd rather be healthy.

THERAPIST: [doubling Alan as
Linda] Well, why can't you be
healthy?

LINDA: [as Alan] Well, if I could,
I would.

THERAPIST: [doubling Alan as
Linda] Uh huh! Sure!

ALAN: [as Linda] If you took
vitamin C, you would be
healthy.

THERAPIST: [doubling Alan as
Linda] You don't take good
care of yourself. You
know . . .

LINDA: [as Alan] If you could
show me an article that says
doctors confirm vitamin C
makes your cold go away I'll
take vitamin C. I took vitamins
before and they never did
anything for me.

ALAN: [as Linda] Even if I
showed you an article, you

wouldn't believe it. You would say the doctor didn't know what he was talking about.

THERAPIST: [doubling as Alan for Linda] And besides that, anything that I have to talk to you about I have to make a whole case, like a lawyer making a presentation. I just want to talk and have you listen and maybe you'd believe me.

LINDA: [as Alan] Well, you're trying to make me believe something that you believe, but I don't believe it.

ALAN: [to therapist] I lost it. I got stuck, maybe because I have a cold.

Joyce, I think adequate doubling has been done for Linda by her husband and you. It's been expanded, so now where are you going with it? I mean, how long are you going to do this?

Well, it's not surprising now that he lost it because Linda has been doubled significantly and is very warmed up to her role. He needs to be placed back in his own role and explain what has come up for him while doing the dialogue. He probably is also having difficulty having his own role mirrored back to him.

THERAPIST: I was wondering when you would say that, because that's not what you would be feeling in response to Linda, right? You usually feel you have to explain to her. I may be wrong.

This is only one aspect of the problem that's occurring. You're not being confrontive in explaining how difficult it is for him to really have her be in the role—as a mirror. You're not exposing Alan's vulnerability and difficulty in having Linda double him.

ALAN: It might be. She doesn't take anything on faith, that I

I think there is a mixing of boundaries here, Joyce. I think know. For some reason, when you said that I flipped out. I agreed with what you were saying, but I wasn't sure if it was from my point of view or hers.

THERAPIST: Right. But she did your role pretty good, huh?

ALAN: Yeah.

THERAPIST: One of the best you've ever heard her do?

ALAN: Yeah, pretty good. I had a pretty good head of steam up and I wasn't feeling good. I was just watching TV and we didn't argue or anything like that.

THERAPIST: Of course, when she said that about a little kiss or something, the old all-too-familiar role you're used to from her rose up. You again felt she was being demanding and not warming you up to her desires.

you are as confused as he is as to what happened here. I think he is able to do her role up to the point when she warms up to it. Once she warms up to his role, he has difficulty staying in her role. This needs to be explored. What's happening?

I think this is an opportunity also to share with Alan that when he role reversals with Linda, he is able to role reverse her old styles of behavior, but none of her new responses. He is unable to reverse roles because he is unsure and has difficulty seeing her change because he is so angry at her old role. Explain how that is understandable and not a performance check, and that not feeling well has nothing to do with his not staying in her role reversal. That at some point there are various reasons why people lose their roles. But let's hear from the couple first. Don't jump in!

ALAN: It wasn't like she wanted a kiss, and would then come over and say "I feel like a kiss." I would give her a kiss, but she comes over and says, "How come you never do that anymore?" And then we start to argue.

THERAPIST: Linda?

Before you turn to Linda, this is a good time to double Alan and allow him to see his own impotency and feelings of never being able to perform effectively. Instead, you're abandoning him. You can ask Linda what she thinks, but not until Alan has been doubled adequately.

LINDA: Well, I don't know. I didn't just say, "How come you don't do that anymore." We were watching a movie and it just looked so nice the way the guy gave the girl . . .

ALAN: But that pisses the shit out of me, when we're watching a movie and you're identifying with the characters in the movie and try to impose their feelings on me. Because I'm not feeling that way when I'm watching the movie. Movies don't give me feelings.

Of course, he's going to be pissed because you haven't doubled him, Joyce. He needs to be doubled.

LINDA: And what does?

ALAN: I don't know, but movies don't. Very rarely.

LINDA: What I want to say without sounding bitchy is you

don't feel that way during a movie, and you don't feel that way ever.

ALAN: That's not what we're talking about.

LINDA: Well, maybe, but . . .

ALAN: We're talking about the movie making you feel one way and I don't feel that way. And instead of trying to make me feel that way, you come over and say, "Well, how come you never feel that way?"

Here is also where you need to double him and say, "I am not you. I have different feelings but that doesn't mean I'm not okay, nor does it mean that you can become hostile to me or that you have a right to become critical of me." You need to double this man, Joyce.

LINDA: I think the movie is making me aware of what I am missing or what I would like.

ALAN: I know it is.

LINDA: But I'm not saying right then and there, "I would like you to lie on me and give me little kisses."

Double here and say "I need your affection, I need your reassurance, I need to feel warmth and love."

ALAN: You came over to me and cuddled next to me and said, "Why don't you ever give me little kisses like that?"

LINDA: It's just a question.

Double him and say, "I feel criticized, I feel overwhelmed, I feel confused, I feel demands made on me."

As a therapist you need to point out that she does not need to defend her statement, that Alan is just telling her how difficult it is for him to respond to her questions, and that perhaps she could make statements, because her questions aren't really questions, they're antagonistic, angry statements.

ALAN: Well, it's a question that I can't answer.

THERAPIST: What you're saying is that you feel demands are being made on you?

ALAN: Yeah.

THERAPIST: To perform?

You need to expand—to perform what? Explain that he needs to perform varied roles. He feels as if he has to perform as a lover, he has to perform as a provider, he has to perform as the breadwinner, and all the other roles that he needs to perform. Linda needs to get a sense of the stress he's under and the inhibition he feels in certain roles.

ALAN: Yeah.

THERAPIST: And you're saying, Linda, that you're not making any demands on him to perform, you're just raising the idea?

LINDA: No, I guess I'm more or less asking out loud.

Where are you going with these statements, Joyce? Do you understand what you're doing? What you really need to do is to double Linda and clarify what she's saying, rather than ask her questions. Double her and she'll correct you if you are wrong.

THERAPIST: You're just reflecting.

LINDA: Well . . .

THERAPIST: I guess it would be more helpful if you said, "Gee, we don't do that anymore."

Joyce, take out the "I guess." Be positive in your statements, affirm them. Just say, "I believe it would be more helpful if you say, 'Gee, we don't do that anymore.'"

LINDA: I don't know if that would have been much better.

THERAPIST: Well, to explain that you're just reflecting on how you're feeling rather than asking him would be making a statement about your feelings rather than making a demand. Or perhaps getting your needs met if you're indeed feeling romantic?

ALAN: See, they don't make movies about 40-year-old people who have been married for eleven years with two kids, the guy's got a cold and they're in therapy and nothing works right. If they made movies like that, then I could identify with them. Anytime you see two people kissing on television or in the movies, it's the first blush of love and their hormones are going all over the place. You can't have that anymore.

THERAPIST: You can't have that anymore?

Double the man! He's saying it's difficult when I've got a cold and I'm tired and I've got two kids and I've been married eleven years. It's difficult to relate to this fantasy movie. Double the man, Joyce. Don't ask him why he can't do that anymore. Show him first how he can find a role in which he can feel fulfilled and expand on. The role in the movie is not doing that for him.

ALAN: No. We had that when we
were dating and that's it. That
was our only shot at it.

THERAPIST: So you're saying that's
gone out of your life.

ALAN: Yeah.

THERAPIST: And what are you
saying, Linda?

You need to expand here on how
he needs to have a role change.

Joyce, before you ask her what
she's saying, correctly double the
man, double Alan and make sure
his feelings are expanded before
you confuse everything by going
to his wife.

LINDA: I'm saying I don't think it
should be gone out of our life.

ALAN: I'm saying I don't want to
be ruled by my hormones.

THERAPIST: You don't want to be
ruled by your hormones?

ALAN: Yeah.

THERAPIST: Those times were
painful and not very good
times in your life?

ALAN: Yeah, like four years ago,
when it scared the shit out of
me.

THERAPIST: Four years ago?

ALAN: Yeah.

THERAPIST: When you had the
affair?

ALAN: Yeah.

THERAPIST: You think it was your
hormones playing tricks on
you then?

ALAN: I sure wasn't acting
rational. Hormones, emotions,
they're all the same thing.
They all come from hormones.

THERAPIST: So the last thing you want is to feel any of that stuff again because you'll be out of control?

ALAN: Right.

THERAPIST: Isn't it possible to find a balance?

ALAN: Yeah. A comfortable feeling.

THERAPIST: A comfortable feeling?

LINDA: Watching TV on one side of the couch with me on the other side.

ALAN: She wants me to be out of control.

I think it would have been a good idea here to double Alan's belief that Linda wants to see him go out of control. Explore what that means to him, maybe by saying, "I feel you want me to lose it just like my dad did when he beat me—you want me to get in touch with my feelings—well, I won't do it, he couldn't make me and you can't make me." Help him expand on what he believes she wants of him in this out-of-control state.

LINDA: I said nothing about being out of control. When you're talking it reminds me of when you say I have two speeds, fast and stop. So what you're saying with hormones is that there's control or nothing.

ALAN: I don't think I have nothing. I may not express it

well, but I don't think I have
nothing.

LINDA: Well, I didn't mean to
insult you, that's the way I
understand it. You don't want
hormones to play any
part . . .

ALAN: What I'm saying is that
when I watch television and
two people kiss I don't have
this desperate feeling that I
have to kiss somebody.

LINDA: I don't either. I don't know
what makes you think I do,
just because I say something.

ALAN: You do it when we're
watching television and
people . . .

LINDA: Well, when am I
supposed to, when we are
eating dinner?

I think it would have been good
here to double her frustration by
saying, "I want to be closer to
you, I want to find ways to relate
to you more intimately, and
sometimes when I see it modeled
on TV or done by other people, it
makes me more aware of what
I'm missing and what we could
have together."

ALAN: Fine, feel that way, but
don't expect me to!

THERAPIST: Linda, are you saying
that you're not really feeling
any special way?

Joyce, this is not the time to ask a
question, this is the time to
double her. She is projecting onto
Alan her inability to connect with
herself, which she calls her desire
to be more intimate. Double her
desire to reduce the sense of

isolation and separation she feels, and the sense of frustration she has at living in a depressed environment similar to her parents and feeling alienated from her very being.

I think you could have doubled for her, Joyce, and said, "I'm somewhat uncomfortable with your refusing to have sex or cuddling. I don't necessarily feel rejected. It doesn't turn me totally off to you."

LINDA: No, not at those particular moments. But there are times, when I feel I would like to kiss you or would definitely like to be kissed. I don't feel like I'm out of control or that I'm at the mercy of my hormones. How many times have I come up to you and said, "I'm horny," and you've said, "I'm not," or "I'm too tired." That's it. I'm all right. I'm not going to jump out the window or anything.

ALAN: [shrugs]

THERAPIST: Well, perhaps what you think she's thinking at the moment and what she's really thinking are not the same. Perhaps, she is just looking to connect with you, not necessarily have sex.

ALAN: There are lots of ways to connect.

LINDA: This is absolutely ridiculous! Would you be insulted if we were watching a movie and they were doing something kinky and I said, "Honey, why don't you suck on my toes anymore?" or something like that. Sometimes

you're just watching a movie
and they're doing something
that isn't a part of your normal
life and you happen to reflect,
"Honey, how come you don't
go skydiving anymore?" You
wouldn't go crazy over that
would you?

ALAN: I never went skydiving. But
it's not the first time in that
context that you've said
something like that and that's
why I got mad.

LINDA: I didn't say, "Alan, how
come you never kiss me
anymore?" I mean I'm just
sitting there watching and I
say . . .

THERAPIST: Let me try to clarify
what is being said. If I'm
wrong you'll let me know.
[turning to Linda] Are you
saying, "Alan, when was the
last time we made love?"

LINDA: Sure, when was the last
time you hugged me, when
was the last time you kissed
me with some kind of passion?

ALAN: When is the last time *you*
kissed *me*, or *you* hugged *me*,
or *you* touched *me* or . . .

LINDA: When was the last time
we even hugged, kissed, or
touched each other or, for that
matter, made love?

ALAN: You tell me how long ago
that was.

LINDA: It was before your cough
and your ear.

ALAN: So you're asking me to do
things that you don't do. You get
pissed off that I don't do them.
Well, you don't do them either.

LINDA: I'm saying that I haven't
done them in two months
because of your being sick all
the time.

ALAN: When was the last time I
hugged you?

LINDA: I don't know, I guess I just
can't answer that one.

ALAN: When was the last time
you hugged me? How many
years ago?

LINDA: You have a bad memory or
else you just don't notice.

THERAPIST: Okay, he just said
that.

Joyce, there's no reason to try to
de-escalate or defuse this
conflict. It seems they're
comparing notes about who's
been giving in the relationship. I
think you need to help them to
double and expand their
aggressive feelings instead of
trying to de-escalate them. To
defuse them is only going to
shove their problems under the
carpet. They are already
proficient at that and that's
certainly not going to resolve the
way they project onto each other,
and try to gain power over each
other, and their avoidance of
vulnerability.

LINDA: Well, he got me mad.

THERAPIST: I know that.

LINDA: And I'm the only one who does hug, I'm the only one who does kiss, other than 7:10 in the morning or 11:15 at night.

ALAN: Kissing me or lying on top of me is not a hug.

Here you could have doubled her and said, "I feel as if I initiate all the affection, and at times when I initiate the affection, it's seen as if I'm wanting sex and that is not what I want. I want affection." You could double him and say, "I feel as if I need to perform; I feel as if I have to fulfill your sexual needs or desires, and that is what overwhelms me and frustrates me."

LINDA: Or rubbing your back or . . .

ALAN: When was the last time you did that?

LINDA: I don't know, maybe I just got tired of it, but I'd say it wasn't more than two months ago.

ALAN: I can't remember the last time.

LINDA: I know, because I don't think you even noticed or if you even remembered. What did I say to you the other day about making love? You said, "I'll have to ask the doctor." You totally forgot what I could be feeling. Then when you came back from the chiropractor and I asked (not that I was in the mood for it), "Did you ask the doctor?" and you said, "What are you talking about?" and I said "What we talked about the other day." You said, "What?" and I said, "Did you ask him about making love?" You repeated, "What are you talking about?"

ALAN: I remember having a conversation with you, where you said something about making love and my thoughts, looking back, were that I doubted if I could have any body motions like that. I don't remember saying that I was going to ask the chiropractor.

THERAPIST: I want to go back to something that I had not heard before. Linda says she's never hugged. However, you're adding that you haven't felt loved or hugged by her?

ALAN: She gives me a hug, or a kiss on a cheek, or a quick rub on the back not because she feels like doing it, but because she wants something in return. When she crawls from the other side of the couch and into my arms and says, "Let's kiss," she's asking something from me.

LINDA: I think it's been a long time since I crawled across the couch and said, "Let's kiss."

ALAN: Well, maybe it has, but . . .

THERAPIST: He's not saying that. He's saying that he thinks you're having a hard time being affectionate or reaching out since he's been sick. This is October, and there was August and September . . .

Well, Joyce, I think it is important for you to clarify what Alan is saying and you seem to be doing that adequately. However, you need to balance your attention by doubling for Linda, demonstrating how she's losing interest even in attempting to connect with him since he was ill.

ALAN: I don't remember her being that way. I won't say she never did it. She isn't overly affectionate. If she wants something, she'll give me a kiss. If she wants to elicit some feeling from me, she'll give me a kiss, in that context. But if I was sitting in a chair, she wouldn't come up to me and put her arms around me and walk away, like the kids do. They come up, grab you from behind, and hold on. If you try to keep them there they'll pull away, you know. They come and then they walk away.

LINDA: I have many a time hugged you . . . and not because I thought that if I hug you, then you'll be good.

ALAN: No, but I'm doing something that brings out that response.

LINDA: When you were feeling really down and lousy about being 40, I can't remember exactly how, but I did comfort you.

ALAN: Yeah, I know, I'm not saying that you've never done it, but you're not overly demonstrative.

LINDA: No, I'm not. I'm not going to say I am, but if I compare myself to you, I am.

THERAPIST: [turning to Linda] So what you're saying is you haven't been calculating your affectionate responses to Alan. I think you needed to add to that, "and I resent and feel angry that you believe I've calculated what I want in order to get you to respond."

LINDA: Yeah, if I had half of what I gave him, I would be ecstatic.

ALAN: I doubt it.

THERAPIST: What do you mean?

ALAN: It's never enough!

LINDA: How do you know?

ALAN: Because you never remember what I do.

LINDA: Well, that could be true, or you just don't . . . so there's nothing for you to remember.

ALAN: You don't see that if I get up and make you a cup of coffee it's exactly the same as if I hug you.

LINDA: No, it isn't the same.

ALAN: And if I make dinner, or go out of my way to do something, it's the same.

LINDA: Not to me, it isn't. Skip the coffee and hug me.

ALAN: Then you would complain about the coffee.

LINDA: No, when was the last time I said anything about the coffee?

ALAN: You haven't.

LINDA: Okay, but I don't know what one thing has to do with another.

THERAPIST: I think he's saying that before you used to complain that he never did things like make the coffee. And now that he's tried to remember to make coffee, you don't acknowledge his attempts to please you.

ALAN: I'm saying that if I spontaneously get up and make coffee, I'm doing something for you, and it's equivalent to a hug.

LINDA: And I'm telling you I'd rather make my own coffee . . . and get a hug.

I think you need to double Linda again. Remember, balance your doubling Alan again and not doubling her by saying, "I need some affection and approval, and at times I need so much affection and approval that I neglect the ways you are trying and I apologize for that. It's my own neediness."

ALAN: You don't appreciate anything I do.

LINDA: That's not true. I appreciate the coffee.

ALAN: But you don't see it for what it is.

LINDA: I don't see it as a hug, I see it as a nice gesture.

THERAPIST: [to Alan] What you're saying is that's your way of giving her a hug. You're not demonstrative.

ALAN: I feel like I want to do something for her and I get up and do it.

THERAPIST: And that comes more natural to you than giving her a hug.

ALAN: Yeah.

THERAPIST: She's asking for a more intimate response.

ALAN: It's being intimate in a manner. I get up, I make coffee, she's feeling good, we sit and drink our coffee together for 15 minutes.

THERAPIST: It feels intimate to you. And then you feel she rejects you.

ALAN: She doesn't reject me when I'm doing it. It happens later when she says, "You never do anything for me." I am what I am, I just express it differently than she does and she doesn't acknowledge it for what it is. She's always saying, "Yeah, that's nice, but I want something else." If I never made coffee again, or if I never made dinner again and came home from work and gave her a hug, pretty soon I would hear, "How come you don't make dinner for me anymore?"

THERAPIST: How does that sound
   to you, Linda?

LINDA: I don't know. To me
   there's no middle ground
   again. It's either never a hug
   and all the coffee you can
   drink or all hugs and nothing
   else. Well, where's the middle
   ground? What about a hug just
   because you feel like it?

ALAN: But I don't get it from you.

LINDA: But you do!

ALAN: When was the last time
   you hugged me?

LINDA: Honey, I didn't mark the
   calendar.

ALAN: Well, I can't remember,
   can you?

LINDA: No, chances are it was
   before your back . . . or your
   cold . . . probably because I
   didn't want to hurt your back
   or catch your cold. Okay, I'm
   going back a few months for
   me, but with you, I'm going
   back a minimum of four years.

ALAN: No.

LINDA: YES!

LINDA: Except for maybe two
   occasions over the years, one
   of which you threw in my face,
   that I didn't want to make love
   in the morning. In the past
   four years, it has been by my
   initiation that we have made
   love.

ALAN: So?

LINDA: So!

ALAN: So, we're not even talking about that, we're talking about hugs.

LINDA: Well, to me they kind of fall into the same category. And you never kiss me passionately, unless we're going to make love, and since you haven't initiated it, except twice over the past four years, you've kissed me with feeling only twice.

ALAN: I'm not a passionate kisser.

LINDA: Can't you practice, or make believe?

ALAN: Well, you don't kiss me passionately either. Just on those rare occasions when . . .

LINDA: [interrupting] Well, still, it's always a lot more than you do.

ALAN: It doesn't matter!

LINDA: To me it does!

ALAN: Whether it's more or less, or who does more or who does less, what matters is that you don't feel intimate and you don't give it out spontaneously or naturally, but you expect me to.

LINDA: I do at times.

ALAN: [loudly] You don't!

THERAPIST: What he's saying is that even if you are, he's not taking it that way.

Joyce, you're doubling for him again, but it isn't enough. If you're going to double for him, you have to double for Linda. Start by doubling Alan and saying, "Since the affair four years ago, I don't feel you truly have forgiven me and are as open and loving as you had been in the past." And then for Linda, you need to say, "Since the affair four years ago our relationship has changed. I feel that I'm not as adequate in making love to you because you don't initiate making love to me and I feel inadequate and not desired as a woman." It's not necessary to tell her at this point that she wants what she didn't get from her mother and that is impossible. Encourage her to reach out to Alan.

LINDA: No, but it's not fair to say that I don't, just because he doesn't see it that way.

ALAN: The same way you don't see it when I do it.

LINDA: When I come next to you on the couch and say, "Let's kiss," we don't have to do anything else, let's just kiss real nice for a couple of minutes.

ALAN: Yeah . . .

LINDA: Yeah, so what? I do it because I enjoy kissing you.

ALAN: Yeah . . .

THERAPIST: Does he respond?

LINDA: Well, he kisses me back.

THERAPIST: Right.

LINDA: I don't know . . . once in a while I would like him to feel it first. I don't know . . . instead of his just responding.

THERAPIST: It sounds like you're asking him to recognize that you have a need and then to fulfill it. And I'm just thinking how nice it is that you're aware of your need. So why not go over and ask him to enjoy what you want to do and see what he does?

Again, Joyce, she doesn't need to be mirrored back. You're mirroring her when she needs to be doubled. What you need to say is, "Since the affair I don't feel wanted and desired by you. And I've forgotten whether it was different before the affair but I need to find other ways to relate to you because these ways don't seem to encourage you to initiate affection or sex with me, and that makes me feel inadequate."

ALAN: You think there's something wrong if you have to do it first? If you ask for it?

LINDA: Well, it's true.

ALAN: I never do it first.

LINDA: It's like if I say, "Alan, bring me roses," why don't you bring me roses? It's different when you tell somebody ten times to bring you flowers or that you like flowers, than for somebody to just pass a flower shop and say, "Hey, that would really be nice," and bring home a bunch as a surprise.

ALAN: I used to bring them home from the A&P, but that wasn't good enough because I didn't go out of my way.

And at the end of that statement, Joyce, you need to double her and say, "Well, perhaps you never had to initiate affection or sex. However, I need to find ways to deal with that because I feel inadequate in inspiring you."

LINDA: You're full of shit, in plain English! Because I always appreciated any flowers that . . .

Joyce, you needed to say as Linda, "I'm angry because you always seem to believe I feel you're inadequate and that I never appreciate anything you do. It gets me angry. And my anger builds up. I don't understand how you can buy me flowers because I've asked for them, but can't seem to think of it yourself. That's what I'm saying. It seems to be a once a lifetime thing. I seem always to be working at trying to express to you what I want, and it always seems that the way I do seems like complaining, and that's not my intention because then I seem to be making you feel inadequate."

ALAN: [interrupting] Yeah, but that's not going to the florist and . . .

LINDA: I never said you had to go to the florist, so I don't know who you're getting that from.

ALAN: Didn't you just say that I don't bring you flowers?

LINDA: Yeah, but I didn't say that it mattered if they came from the A&P or the florist.

ALAN: Well, that's because I got them from the A&P.

LINDA: When was the last time?

ALAN: It hasn't been for a while.

LINDA: I appreciated them when you brought them from the A&P. And I didn't say that you

never do, I'm just trying to
make an analogy of having to
ask for flowers and getting
them is nice, and asking for a
kiss and getting one is nice,
but it's just a little bit nicer
when somebody gives you a
kiss because he wants to, and
not because he was asked.

ALAN: But I give you things
because I want to. I just don't
give you kisses.

Beginning of Closure

THERAPIST: I'm going to interject
for a moment. I'm happy that
you two are at last having an
argument. You haven't talked
like this in months. You may
not resolve this, but at least
you're back to connecting with
each other in a dialogue.

ALAN: We had an argument this
weekend.

THERAPIST: Well, you must be
feeling better, or she thinks
you feel better.

ALAN: Oh, I don't know. Strange
things happen at the onset of a
cold.

THERAPIST: [laughing] Linda,
you've been sitting here for
weeks just listening.

LINDA: Because I've been letting
him do all the talking.

THERAPIST: Because . . .

LINDA: Because I told him, you

don't talk to me at home. At
least I get to hear what's going
on in your mind here. And I
know a lot has been on your
mind. That's why I've been
quiet.

ALAN: I haven't neglected you.

LINDA: I didn't say you did. I'm
just stating the facts. I'm not
expecting anything from you.

THERAPIST: But I think it's good
for you to listen to him so you
can get a sense of how he's
feeling. At the same time, I
think you've been bottling up
your own feelings, not knowing
how to connect with him.

LINDA: I was not aware that I was
bottling up resentment
towards him.

THERAPIST: Well, perhaps you
haven't been, but this is the
first week in a long time that I
have heard you express
yourself.

ALAN: Well, I've been depressed
for a long time. As a matter of
fact, I've been depressed all
my life.

THERAPIST: Oh, you were, huh?

Instead of saying, "Oh, you were,
huh?" I think you could
acknowledge his awareness that
he has been depressed and his
courage is expressing his
depression, thereby encouraging
Linda to realize that in many
ways he reminds her of how

depressed her own parents have been, especially her mother, and how depressed she has been, and unaware that when Alan is severely depressed at times, and has been so recently. Linda attempts first to rescue him, then withdraws from him, and finally becomes hostile toward him.

LINDA: I don't know why you were depressed.

ALAN: Well, I have a cold so I feel even worse. I'm tired and I'm dragged out. The bank has more problems now because of what they did last week.

LINDA: What did they do last week?

ALAN: They showed a loss for the last quarter and they won't be able to pay a dividend.

THERAPIST: Well, we're out of time. Let's bring this subject back next week.

Before going on to deeper explication of a couple's psychotherapeutic session using AMP, an in-depth explanation of the AMP rules is required and explained in the following chapter.

8

ᘒ

Rules for Applying AMP

$\mathcal{R}$ules for AMP demand that the enactment take place in the here and now, no matter when the original conflict occurred (or even if it never occurred). In order to mend distortions and dysfunctional imbalances, the couple has to reintegrate the experiences or perceptions at a new level. Role reversal accomplishes this by enabling the protagonist to reexperience, redigest, and reintegrate these experiences and grow beyond their negative impact, thereby becoming more spontaneous.

THE USE OF SOCIOMETRY

As humans, we desire to be affiliated, and choose affiliates based on the criteria of our selection process. An individual's creativity, productivity, and ability to express fulfilling roles with others is dependent on his or her ability to maintain fluid intimate mutual relationships with some psychological satisfaction. When looking at the psychological satisfaction of a couple in psychotherapeutic treatment, as noted earlier, the therapist using sociometry examines the choice patterns of the couple—the criteria each partner has used to select each other and the reciprocity present in their choice. Questions the couples AMP therapist explores to learn information about the couple's sociometric patterns include:

Who chose whom in this relationship?
Was it reciprocal?
What were the criteria for choices?
Were the criteria reciprocal?

Indeed, some aspects of an individual's sociometry also develop from his or her parents' or even grandparents' selection patterns (Siroka-Dubbs 1990). Each partner comes to the relationship with his or her own sociometric imprint—a sociometric position inscribed earlier in their family of origin. Questions for the therapist to ask each partner when working with a couple to explore generation sociometric patterns include:

How did your parents meet?
Did your parents chose each other as partners?
Why did your parents choose to have you as a child?
How were you accepted by the family when you were born?
What roles did your parents use in their relationship with each other and with you?

When the therapist finds answers to these indicating the role patterns of each partner, the psychodramatic techniques of AMP can then come into play. This enables each partner to develop a more expansive role repertoire, and capture or mirror the non-reciprocal telic relationship he or she once had with a parent. If the individual as a child received mixed messages, such as "I love you, but," he is more likely to choose a partner with whom he does not have a reciprocal positive tele. The next vignette demonstrates how a partner is affected by their parent's style of relating.

In the middle of their session, Jane and Pete developed aspects of a ritualistic conflicting warm-up they have:

PETER: [turning to Jane] You sound just like my mother.

JANE: Don't say that. I'm nothing like your mother.

THERAPIST: [turning to Peter] Let's see how that statement takes place in action. Pete, reverse roles and show Jane what triggers that feeling and statement from you.

PETER: [as Jane] [reversing seats with Jane and moving into her posture] I don't have to explain how I spent that money.

THERAPIST: [turning to Peter] Please reverse roles back to your original posture. Now tell me, in your earlier life, did you hear or experience a similar aggressive statements about money, perhaps in your childhood?

PETER: My parents always argued about money.

THERAPIST: Jane, will you take the role of Peter's mother?

JANE: [reluctantly] Okay.

Although the choice of using a mate in a negative transference role is usually avoided, Peter in this instance was explaining how Jane already fits the role.

THERAPIST: Okay, Peter, show us how your parents' arguments about money would occur. Take the role of your dad relating to your mother about an incident related to money. Go over and pick a scarf or object from the pile and put it on.

PETER: [wearing a beret, as his father, takes the seat and turns to his wife, Sarah, played by Jane] You can't spend money on clothes like you do. I don't have money for the rent this month because of your spending. You're like one of the kids. [in a dismissing gesture] I'm disgusted with you.

THERAPIST: [interrupting the scene] Peter, let me take the role of your dad. Sit over there and observe.

PETER: [puzzled] Okay.

THERAPIST: [stepping into Peter's dad's role, putting the beret on and repeating the same dialogue to Sarah as Peter's mother]

JANE: [as Peter's mother] [repeating and exaggerating the tone, volume, and dialogue]

THERAPIST: [standing up when the scene is completed, turning to Peter] Okay, now please reverse roles back with me. Put the beret back in the pile in the corner. [after their original positions are assumed] Now, tell me, what was your reaction to observing that scene?

PETER: [somewhat hesitantly] You sounded like my dad talking to my mother, which means when I speak to Jane about money I must sound like my father. Wow!

Another example of sociometry. Sociometry illuminates the criteria, the attributes an individual considers important in his or her choice of affiliations and associates in specific situations or instances. These choices of affiliations come out of an individual's belief system as explained below.

PERSONAL BELIEFS

Beliefs or personal constraints pertaining to a role are the elements least likely to emerge directly in an enactment (Williams 1989, p. 66). Since they are interactive, their meaning or function becomes clear only when the action is observed; therefore, nearly all the information needed by the therapist may be derived from questioning the partner about the context and behavior of the roles. The beliefs of a role are the most complex aspects of role assessment for the therapist because they are largely composed of attitudes, assumptions, projections, convictions, and expectations that restrain an individual from taking action. Once the roles are warmed up, interviews about beliefs can take place.

BELIEFS

Prior to the initiation of action in a session, a brief interview by the therapist illuminates the selected auxiliary's belief system as the partner presenting the drama is interviewed in the auxiliary role, as shown in the following excerpt:

> ANN: [turning to the therapist] My mother is unhappy that Rick refuses to keep the family ritual of dinner at her house on Sundays. I feel so conflicted. I can understand that Rick has to work on Saturday and would like to relax at home on Sunday, but my mother gets offended so easily. I hate to see her so unhappy.
>
> RICK: [jumping in] That woman is always interfering in our lives.
>
> THERAPIST: [turning to Rick] I would like you to witness Ann's difficulty with her mother. Perhaps then you will have a clear understanding of the problem and then we can both help Ann.
>
> RICK: I don't know what good it will do, but okay.
>
> THERAPIST: [turning to Ann] Ann, I would like you to bring your mother here. Go over to that pile of odds and ends in the corner [a pile of folded pieces of material of various colors and textures] and pick an accessory to wear while representing your mother, then take a seat in that other chair. Make sure when you sit there that you take your mother's posture and use her gestures. [After Ann had picked a black piece of material to drape over her shoulders she sat down in the seat provided for her mother.]
>
> THERAPIST: [turning to Ann in the role of her mother] Thank you for joining Rick and Ann today. I'm sorry, I think I missed your name.
>
> ANN: [as her mother] Oh, I'm not surprised you don't know my name. Rick doesn't seem to remember it either. He keeps

calling me Mom. I'm not his mom! He calls me Mom and then treats me like a stranger.

This interview helped Rick see how his behavior towards Ann's mother needed to be evaluated and changed. On one hand, he called her "Mom," but had little if any warmth toward her in his verbal or nonverbal communication. This is an example of how a person's belief system becomes externalized.

BEHAVIOR

The therapist using AMP is interested in the sequence of behaviors that link one action to another, as well as the sequence of events that occurs, as shown in the following example.

Mary had stated in the couples sessions with her husband, Barry, that she had been depressed and feeling asexual since the birth of their daughter, when her mother-in-law moved in to help. The couples therapist, using AMP, took the couple back in time to concretely view the behavioral changes Mary believed had taken place when her mother-in-law moved in, and set the scene, beginning with the concept of time.

> THERAPIST: Mary, what time frame are we discussing? How many years ago was your daughter born? Let's go back to that year. You are just coming home from the hospital with Barry. Move over to the other chair and let's establish your role during that time frame. Mary, how old are you?
> MARY: Twenty-nine.
> THERAPIST: How do you feel about having a new baby girl?
> MARY: Okay.
> THERAPIST: Mary, go behind your chair and double your inner feelings.
> MARY: [from behind the seat] I'm [hesitantly] scared I won't be able to take care of her.

THERAPIST: [standing up with that knowledge established] Come here, Mary. [taking her hand] Let's move forward in time to one month after you are home with the baby. [pointing to the scarves] Take a scarf from the pile over there and hold your baby. What is her name?

MARY: Suzie.

THERAPIST: How are you adjusting to motherhood?

MARY: I'm nervous a lot. Mom and Barry seem to take over. They know so much more about what Suzie needs. Suzie doesn't seem relaxed when I hold her. Mom always knows how to calm her down.

Mary's perceptions of the relationship with Barry and her mother-in-law since the birth of their daughter became slowly concretized. Serving as a witness/participant aided Barry in both understanding and empathizing with his wife's perception.

Behaviors make up the role context a person assumes in relationship to others, as shown below.

ESTABLISHING ROLE CONTEXT

The references to time and place in relation to oneself and to significant others is established within the context of the individual client's point of view. Establishing the contextual role framework of an individual is exemplified in the following recollection scene:

THERAPIST: Sue, you have spoken of your mother's interference several times. Let's set a scene in which an interaction of this type occurs. [taking her hand and moving to the center of the room, walking and talking] Where are we? Who is here with you?

SUE: [slowly in thought] Well, my mother is on the phone with my sister.

THERAPIST: Is anyone else here?

SUE: Yes, my grandmother is sitting in the kitchen with us.

THERAPIST: Okay, your grandmother is here as well. Reverse roles and take your grandmother's role, please.

SUE: [as grandmother] [goes over to the pile of extras, takes a scarf, moves to a chair over to the right, and sits down with her arms folded.]

INTERVIEWING IN A ROLE

An important guideline for the AMP couples therapist is to explore what role exists, who is affected by the roles performed, how and by whom the roles are responded to, and what happens next, as in the following:

THERAPIST: Let's see if we can get a clearer picture of the problem. Would you mind, Jeff, serving as a witness here so you can better understand Sandra's dilemma?

JEFF: [hesitantly] Okay.

THERAPIST: This offers an opportunity to have Sandra bring her mother into the office so we can get to know her.

SANDRA: [somewhat reluctantly] I guess so.

THERAPIST: Sandra, go over to the group of accessories in the corner of the room and pick one to add to your mother's role, and then take a seat over there with it.

SANDRA: [as her mother] [takes the chair provided, wearing a black veil over her face]

THERAPIST: Excuse me, I believe I have not met you. I'm Sandra's and Jeff's therapist. I don't believe I know your name.

SANDRA: [as her mother] I'm not surprised you don't know my name. Sandra doesn't want anything to do with me since she married Jeff. Jeff has turned her thinking. My name is Gloria. Do you think he calls me Gloria? No! He calls me Mom. I'm not his mom and I don't want to be. I have one daughter, and I had one son, but he's gone. And if this young man thinks he is going to take my Bobby's place he is mistaken.

THERAPIST: Thank you, Gloria, you have been most helpful. Sandra, please reverse roles.

Observing this interview with Sandra in her mother's role enabled Jeff to express his empathy and understanding for Sandra's mother and for Sandra's concern about her mother as well. He and Sandra continued a discussion of what ways would best aid them.

When using Action Modality Psychotherapy with a couple, it is important when moving one of the partners into action that you interview him or her for that role. This requires the therapist to ask specific questions and set the stage.

What are the significant others and role relationships?
Who is most upset by the problem?
Who feels helpless, and to whom do they appeal?

Moreno would refer to this process as an inquiry into the *status nascendi*, focusing on how something grows and evolves.

As Bateson (1979) noted, the context of a role reveals to another the individual's reaction in a specific time frame. One way the therapist can ascertain this is to ask, "What is happening in this particular scene? To whom are you talking? Who else is there? What does this other person think of what is happening?" This type of questioning will keep the action concise and well timed. At times a role takes place within a context that adds surplus to reality, as explained below.

SURPLUS REALITY USED WITH AMP

Surplus reality is another technique used in AMP, where the therapist increases and expands the reality impact of the situation, offering the protagonist the opportunity to reexperience a difficult situation, and a chance to correct his or her reactions. Scenes that reflect a client's early childhood situations, where he or she had to act differently or suppress emotions in order to survive, can be reenacted. The partner can be brought into the scene to represent someone who was there at the time, such as a mother, sibling, or aunt. Roles can be expanded, intensified, and overplayed in AMP to include all aspects of surplus reality. An empty chair is another tool frequently used in AMP to represent an absent significant other, or someone with whom the partner is currently interacting. This way of organizing the data allows the individual presenting the situation, with the assistance of the therapist, to create a new reality with his or her partner and an opportunity to reframe the problem and its solution. The *extension* or *surplus reality* is not an imitation or reflection of reality but a means of having each partner play out the feelings and perceptions of the mate to unite each with the affect and individual views of the therapeutic situation.

Surplus reality in couples work enables the therapist to assist the couple in experiencing the psychodramatic reality of the represented mate's (protagonist's) perception of a real or imagined situation. This may include an exploration with the self, as shown in the following vignette. Mitch and Sally had arrived at the session late.

SALLY: [sitting down and turning to Mitch] Mitch was running late leaving work.

MITCH: I really did not want to come tonight. It has been a hell of a day. I didn't sleep well. I had a dream from which I feel like I never really woke up. It sounds silly, but I had a dream there was a monster following me and I couldn't get away. I tried, but it was hopeless.

THERAPIST: [turning to Mitch] Interesting. Let's recreate the scene. Reverse roles and show us the monster. [facing the pile of scarves at the corner of the room] Use one of those scarves to drape over yourself for the role.

At times the therapist or the mate may take the role of an auxiliary as occurred in this case. The auxiliary role was taken by the therapist so that any negative feelings or thoughts related to the role would not be transferred onto his mate.

THERAPIST: [pointing to the floor] Now take the body position of the monster and show us.

MITCH: [takes the orange scarf from the pile, drapes it over his head, and kneels down on all fours]

THERAPIST: [addressing Mitch in the role of the monster] Who are you?

MITCH: [gruffly] I'm his fear.

THERAPIST: How long have you been around?

MITCH: [as monster] Forever and ever.

THERAPIST: Does Mitch know about you?

MITCH: [as monster, angrily] He tries to ignore me, but [loudly] I will not be ignored. I [louder] get bigger and bigger. He can't get away from me!

THERAPIST: Thank you for joining us, monster. Is there anything you want us to know?

MITCH: [as monster] You already know. I just told you, [louder] don't ignore me.

THERAPIST: Okay, monster. Mitch, reverse roles. [turning to Mitch, who has returned to his seat] I would like you to think about the monster a minute. [after a somewhat long pause] Do you at times feel like a monster with Sally?

MITCH: [with some thought] Yes, I do, but only once in a while.

THERAPIST: [turning to Mitch] Tell Sally what it's like being with her at times. I'll assist by doubling.

MITCH: [nods and proceeds]

This exercise assisted Mitch in explaining how he moves into a passive/aggressive stance, or role position with Sally when he wants to please her. At this point, the couple was able to further discuss situations in which their dysfunctional role positions become established. They then gained understanding of each other's behaviors and fears.

The contextual framework of roles, and the surplus reality within which they are developing, is established in the setting of the scene, establishing the space, time, and persons related to the scene.

SCENE SETTING

Part of warming up the subject further to an enactment, an encounter, is established through scene setting. The time, place, and person in the here and now are established, as in the following segment:

RICH: [to the therapist] I don't understand her.

THERAPIST: [moving into the near doubling position] That must be very frustrating.

RICH: Yeah!

THERAPIST: [turning to Jane] Did you know that Rich didn't understand your response to him the other day?

JANE: Sort of. He didn't say much.

THERAPIST: [turning to the couple] Okay, let's try this. I want you to both go back to the time the incident we are discussing took place and talk to each other in the here and now. I will move behind each of you and double your statements as needed. To start let's set the scene. What day is it? Where are you both? Set up that corner of the room as it is needed for the scene. Who is there? Now, what time was it? What is happening?

RICH: It was Tuesday evening. The kids had just left the dinner table.

JANE: [nodding] I thought it was Wednesday.

RICH: No, it was Tuesday. I had to get the garbage out to the curb.

JANE: [quietly, in agreement] Oh, yeah.

THERAPIST: [summarizing in a desire to further concretize the scene] Okay, both of you are at the dinner table, it is Wednesday evening, and the kids have just left the table. Rich, position the chairs as if you are at the table and start the dialogue as it took place then.

Auxiliaries, extra individuals (often family members), may be included as part of a person's drama, as explained below.

CHOOSING AUXILIARIES AS FAMILY MEMBERS

Peter and Adele were halfway through the couples session when:

PETER: [turning to the therapist] This is crazy. I can hear my mother's voice in my head right now.

THERAPIST: Peter, that is not unusual. We often take the shapes of auxiliaries from our life.

PETER: [perplexed] Well, that's interesting, because sometimes I think Adele sounds just like my father.

THERAPIST: [turning to Peter] Can you show us? Set the scene so we can place Adele in your father's role. Where are your parents having this dialogue?

PETER: In the living room.

THERAPIST: Set up the room.

PETER: [standing up and establishing the setting]

THERAPIST: Now, where does your father sit?

PETER: [gesturing over the to left] He always sits over there by the TV.

THERAPIST: Okay, take his position.

PETER: [taking his father's position]

THERAPIST: [interviewing Peter in the role of his father, extending a handshake] Henry, it's nice to meet you. [after further introductory dialogue] Tell me, how are you and your wife getting along?

This type of scene continues until it reaches a climax, at which time the therapist would have Adele and Peter repeat the scene, with Adele taking Peter's wished-for dad's position with his mother (played by Peter). This would be followed with Adele taking a wished-for position in their relationship today. Then Adele would receive role training from Peter in the role he wished she would take with him. A follow-up discussion or summing up, with each partner sharing how they felt in the role, the familiarity they have with the role from their past, and how the role would benefit them today, would offer closure.

THE USE OF METAPHOR

The couples therapist may create a shift in an enactment by concretizing a metaphor. For example, if one of the partners is stuck, the therapist may ask, "What is the *essence* of the relationship you are trying to share with us?" Or, to heighten the emotional tone of an interaction, the therapist may ask one of the partners to sculpt his or her body to represent his or her feeling or to express his or her reaction to what has come before. This lends an "as-if-ness" to the situation, with more color and verisimilitude, because the significant other is being portrayed by the partner. At one point in a session, Alan told me how "dead tired" he felt in the marriage. He took the position of "dead tired," which was then expanded through doubling. Alan was then able to express to Linda how his assumed role of the doctor in the marriage was draining him.

TRAINING THE PARTNERS
TO DOUBLE EACH OTHER

Part of therapy is training couples in how to double, an important useful skill each mate can carry over into daily living. An example of this type of training takes place in the following vignette. Bill and Nancy entered the office together, laughing.

> NANCY: [sitting down and smiling across at the therapist] Well, I'll start. Our son Jim is getting away with murder. Bill always gives into whatever he wants. Now it's a new car for his birthday, which is ridiculous. I haven't said anything to Bill because I didn't want to start anything. I know he wouldn't get it.
>
> THERAPIST: [turning to Bill] Bill, without telling me more about this for now, do you believe you understand Nancy's feelings?
>
> BILL: [glancing at the therapist, he nods his head]
>
> THERAPIST: Okay. Let me explain what I would like to try. So far in our sessions I have been doing the "doubling" for each of you. As I explained a few weeks ago, when I started I was taking the doubling role by going behind each of you, speaking in the first person as if I were you, and stating what I believed to be your inner feelings, which you then could correct or expand.
>
> BILL: [nodding in agreement]
>
> NANCY: I think so.
>
> THERAPIST: During times when I have doubled, I've gotten out of my seat and gone behind each of you and articulated what I believed your inner feelings to be. Now, Bill, I would like you to go behind Nancy, and in the first person say what you believe Nancy is thinking or feeling about your offering your son Jim a car. Don't worry about getting it just right. She will correct you if you're wrong.
>
> BILL: [nodding in agreement] Sure.

THERAPIST: [turning to Nancy] I would like you to listen and correct or expand what Bill says.

NANCY: Okay!

BILL: [as Nancy's double, behind Nancy's chair] I can't believe you would offer Jim a car without speaking to me first. But I better keep my mouth shut before there's more trouble. Jimmy will think I don't want him to have a car.

NANCY: Yeah. How could you play up to our own son like that? I think you are afraid to get him angry.

THERAPIST: [turning to Bill] Bill, please sit down and respond to Nancy's comment to you.

BILL: [sitting down, turning to Nancy]

THERAPIST: Nancy, please repeat your last statement so Bill can respond again.

NANCY: I think you are afraid of Jimmy and want to be the good guy, which infuriates me.

BILL: [somewhat reticently] I didn't think it out. I always wanted my father to offer me a car when I was 17. I had to earn my own car, which took me until I was 21.

Bill's doubling of Nancy aided him in developing empathy for her, gave him insight into his behavior, and validated Nancy. Nancy, rather than withholding her feelings, which usually turned into resentment toward her husband, was able to enter into a discussion with Bill about the incident. This completed, they could then encounter each other, as explained below.

ENCOUNTER

The importance of interacting with another is explained in Moreno's notion and principle of *encounter*. The encounter entails two or more persons meeting "not only to face one another, but to live and experience one another as actors, each in his or her own right"

(Moreno 1956, p. 13). The encounter is considered the primary form of all synergistic human relations, "a realization of the self through the other" (Moreno 1956, p. 13), bridging the distance to another. The impact of the meeting is both self-confirming and self-transcending for each person. In couples work, the therapist enhances each partner's ability to encounter the other.

Exploring the sociometry of the couple through the use of sociometric means such as psychodrama, improves the couple's ability to encounter and relate with one another, as exemplified in the vignettes above.

OTHER TECHNIQUES

Some other techniques used in Action Modality Psychotherapy may include:

Soliloquy—a monologue by one partner.

Therapist's Soliloquy—unspoken monologue by the therapist of hidden thoughts and feelings of a mate.

Self-Presentation—a partner presents him- or herself, his or her parent, sibling, and any significant other.

Multiple Double—several doubles of a partner, each portraying a different aspect.

Future Projection—a mate's portrayal of how he or she believes the future to be, complete with time, place, and person.

Retraining—when one mate tries out a new role.

These techniques are presented throughout the transcripts included in the following chapters.

TRANSFERENCE IN COUPLES THERAPY

Couples in a long-term intimate relationship share a common mystery, a mysterious history that combines life situations, cultural situations, and family events that have been touched by the same experience. Often in such a mysterious, deeply emotional relationship, parts of the self that are disowned become projected onto the partner. It is the aim of the therapist to reincorporate all such projected roles in a process that requires endurance, tenacity, patience, and continual review, as will be seen in the following session. Transference thus becomes the psychological branch of tele or empathy.

AMP enables a couple to make their information compact, expand their perceptions, and evoke and express emotions that could not otherwise be expressed, by means of concretization and dramatization. As soon as the self (or part of the self) becomes an outside object or another person, it is concretized; as action takes form, it is dramatized. When a couple is talking about an event, it is usually impossible for them to control both the interaction and the emotional impact of the event. However, when they get into the scene created by the therapist in co-action with them, the as-if-ness of the experience becomes more pronounced and they begin to shape, think, and feel as they did (or would have) in the actual situation. The physical and verbal cues become maximized and feed into the interaction with the therapist. Auxiliaries (partner or therapist) physically change places with the presenting mate and repeat the words that his or her partner spoke so the partner can hear his or her own words while in the role of the other. By taking the role of the other, the auxiliary position broadens his or her experience, and thereby gains a deeper understanding of the other, and expresses him- or herself in ways he or she would normally avoid.

The aspects of sociometric attraction and repulsion have underpinnings for many aspects of living and relating. The telic phenomenon, the social atom, psychodrama, and role theory are aimed at having the couple develop an ability to encounter each other. All are key concepts of sociometry utilized in AMP couples work.

THE COUPLES THERAPIST WARM-UP

As the couples therapist warms up to using AMP with a couple, he or she needs to keep several points in mind:

1. The *purpose* of the session, that is, the purpose for the couple. What do they expect individually, and as a unit?
2. What is the *role* the couple wants you to assume and what is the role you are comfortable with?
3. What *structure* will you use? Are you comfortable with applying AMP? Are there other styles that you want to add?
4. What *process* will you use? Do you intend to introduce certain techniques of AMP? Do you need to warm up the couple to specific AMP tools? Will you provide a warm-up and cool-down (closure)?

Elements of scene setting to be carried out before warming-up to applying AMP:

1. Set a *time* with the couple or mate as to when the original situation occurred.
2. Set the *place/space*.
3. Set the *roles*. Who was there? What were they doing? How were the movements performed?
4. Get some sense of the *conflict* in your own mind—a hypothesis of the conflict.
5. Develop these elements and move them into *action* in the here and now.

If the argument took place six years ago, go back in time and develop the action as if it were occurring now.

Having a further understanding of the rules of AMP, including the therapist warm-up to the process, we will now explore an AMP session with the therapist's process and evaluation.

CHAPTER

9

᠕

Therapist's AMP
Evaluation Approach:
Another Session

WARM-UP TO SESSION, APRIL 21

After reviewing the last few video sessions and discussing this couple, I decided to change my opening approach. Over the last nine months of their treatment, I had assumed a somewhat laid-back warm-up and waited for either partner to initiate the session's dialogue. Two weeks prior, I had discussed my frustration with this couple, to no avail. I explained that I had felt overwhelmed lately by their continuous battling. They appeared to have no interest in working their problems through toward a solution. Each seemed to have a set view of what I was to hear and validate. Their progress over the last month seemed blunted. I began to feel as if I were trying to mediate one of my parents' arguments. I felt my anxiety growing as I thought about speaking to them about my concerns. The more warmed up I became, the more concerned I felt about their ineffective use of their joint session time. When I analyzed my own feelings, I realized I was afraid they would become angry and possibly quit therapy as they had with their last therapist. I had all I could do to contain my anxiety. I wanted to flee. Aware of how I was feeling, I decided to open the session with a statement about my concerns.

Session Dialogue	Therapist Soliloquy	Therapist Reflection
THERAPIST: I have a comment. I watched the tape from last week's session and then I watched the tape from the previous session, and before that I watched the tape we viewed last week of an earlier session, and I'm feeling like somehow we are playing games. I don't feel both of you are working on this relationship to make it better, to try to improve it. Watching the video tapes is not going to help a whole lot unless there are some changes made, unless some learning from the process takes place.	I entered the office where they were already seated, greeted them, and turned on the video. Alan, as usual, was wearing his pinstriped suit, with the tie removed, while Linda was wearing a pair of casual jeans and a simple blouse from her day of house and childcare chores. Before I get caught up in their process, let me say what's on my mind.	

For the last month the couple had been viewing the initial opening warm-up of their previous session. They had asked if they could view the tapes. Alan initiated the suggestion and Linda agreed. I had decided to use viewing of the last half of the previous videotaped session as a warm-up to the current session. In addition, I suggested that they move their session to the end of my workday and meet for a 90-minute session instead of 50 minutes, to allow time for viewing the previous session.

THERAPIST: You're spending your money and my time to help you do what?

ALAN: [looking somewhat startled] I don't know what you mean. When we fight, it's shorter in duration.

THERAPIST: [questioning] You think so? [turning to Linda] Do you agree?

I'm amazed he doesn't agree with me.

LINDA: Yes.

ALAN: [interrupting] I think we have changed the way we treat each other.

How can he find something positive in this relationship?

THERAPIST: You feel that you are arguing differently?

LINDA: We fight less than we did back when we started therapy. I'm usually able to get out of it. However, I also feel that many times things are saved up for the nights when we're here.

They have been very punctual and dedicated to getting to their sessions. They have a sitter for the children and even a backup sitter.

ALAN: We still have a basic problem. And that is we need a third party to mediate. That is the basis of our problem.

Okay, that makes sense. They need me to validate their points of view.

THERAPIST: After we reviewed the previous session together, you told me that viewing the session did not help you resolve your problem at all. We discussed Linda's reaction to your smoking. [turning to Alan] I didn't feel there was any resolution, did you?

Something seems to be happening that makes these sessions more intense.

Well, for one thing, I am very warmed up to my issue, that I'm doing all the work for this relationship. However, the effort it takes to warm them up seems too challenging. They seem to require continual warming up from me. I'm having difficulty being a catalyst and I've been hiding my own frustration.

ALAN: No.

THERAPIST: I observed you both watching the video. You were more angry at each other on the second go-around and were interacting with each other with greater hostility.

Boy, do I sound outspoken!

ALAN: I don't recall. The issue definitely was not resolved, so it's something that we have to work on.

Press on. Everything is still up in the air. He doesn't have a clue as to how many steps are involved in changing. He makes it sound so easy. If it is that easy, then why haven't they done it?

THERAPIST: Was it discussed at home during the week?

I continually avoid getting Alan angry. Why don't I ask him what he meant by work and when he intends to begin?

I have taken responsibility for keeping this relationship together. My countertransferential issues are being activated. Both of these people are in many ways too immature for marital therapy, where they might learn communication skills. The role of the double for each other, for example, requires that they be able to reverse roles and improve the way they address each other. What I'm really doing here is managing two childish individuals, especially Linda. This situation activates my experience with my own parents. My mother was childish and I took the adult role. However, they seem to be hearing me or at least talking to each other now about what they've gained in therapy. And I'm experiencing some role relief.

ALAN: No.

THERAPIST: You benefit from coming here by having someone mediate between you?

Let me mirror back what he said, so I'm sure I've got his message.

ALAN: Yeah. At least there is some relief.

THERAPIST· Assuming there is no arguing going on here in the session.

What kind of relief? Do they realize how much bickering they do here?

That's interesting. It's as if they experience relief and I feel the burden. I'm developing role fatigue, just as they do in their relationship.

ALAN: . . . and there is listening going on.

LINDA: I mean, my first thought was, I don't listen to him, so at least you listen to him.

I'm getting tired of listening. He's your husband.

THERAPIST: Is that what you noticed?

LINDA: [reflecting] After I said that, I thought to myself, well, he doesn't listen to me, but at least Joyce hears me. Here is my need to be heard and I think that is why we can't argue.

What about your role? What do you notice of yourself, Linda?

This statement emphasizes my sense that the most I can do for this couple is to listen and double each of them, validate their experience, and provide role training by serving as a role model. Neither one seems to be able to listen to the other and support individual growth in some way. They say they're arguing less, so some doubling and validating on my part must be getting through.

ALAN: [pointedly] I disagree. I hear you!

LINDA: [smirking] Yeah. Ha, ha!

ALAN: No. [loudly] I hear you, but I don't know how to deal with what I'm hearing. You don't listen, I listen but I don't know how to deal with what I hear.

Okay, that's a good observation. Let's take it further.

THERAPIST: Is that in part because you feel overwhelmed . . . that it reminds you of how it was for you as a child with your father?

ALAN: Well, I think the problem is that when I'm confronted with something, it's impossible for me to say anything because she isn't listening. It doesn't get through, so I become extremely frustrated. [turning to Linda, fearfully] You wanted to continue to argue on the way home last week. I had to say over and over that I didn't want to talk about it.

I could have done some role training here and explained to Linda that she would do best to double Alan before she mirrors him.

THERAPIST: You said you don't want to talk about it. This is what I'm talking about. How are things going to change if there is no discussion?

Poor woman, she is being continually rejected, but she still attacks.

I see that Alan wanted to break the cycle. Perhaps if I had explained to him that he could validate Linda without agreeing with her by doubling her, he could find a more helpful way to discontinue the faulty communication, or I could have suggested another alternative, such as telling him he could suggest they resume their discussion at a later time.

ALAN: I don't want to perpetuate the argument. That's her point of view. I haven't changed my mind and come to her point of view, which is what she wants. That's impossible, and the other way around, her agreeing with my view, is also impossible.

LINDA: [angrily] I don't like your saying I was trying to get you to change your mind. [sharply] I don't think I can do that.

ALAN: [harshly] Well, why perpetuate the argument?

Wow, he sounds angry.

LINDA: I don't even remember, perhaps because I felt it wasn't resolved. I can't just close a book and say okay, we'll return to it in two weeks.

Here they go. I feel like I'm at a ping-pong match and I'm supposed to be the referee.

Yes, she's unable to let go. I would prefer to see her individually so we could work on some of her strong feelings of rage and release them. Perhaps I could encourage her to do some individual work in front of him. I have difficulty getting him to do any individual work in front of her because she tends to shame him at these times. However, I also realize that his rage, the hostility in his voice, frightens me, too. I end up focusing on Linda and avoiding my own experience. I should double his rage. I should double Linda's possible fear of his rage, but instead I'm focusing on Linda, which is how it was for me as a child. I always focused on my mother's inadequacies, never on my father's.

ALAN: But it's impossible to resolve it that way. You're trying to convince me that you have a valid viewpoint.

LINDA: But why? Maybe I just want you to know that I do have a valid viewpoint and it may not be the same as . . .

ALAN: [interrupting loudly] That's the whole point! You don't want to talk about the problem, you want me to know.

LINDA: But can't two people have a valid viewpoint? So what's wrong with me wanting you to understand?

How can I get her to hear what he's saying?

I can see now how I again detached myself from my fear of aggression in Alan's voice. I just detach and move to focusing on Linda, where I feel safe.

ALAN: [raising his voice and interrupting] Because I heard it, and I disagree with it, and you can't change that, so why keep having the same argument? It's not about that.

Now he's getting agitated.

He seems to be able to get the message to me that it's too hot and we better focus on Linda. I'm reinforcing their reaction to his rage. They're fearful of his rage and so am I. I can't double him if I'm hiding from myself and my feelings. I need to use my inner feelings to double each of them. I'm stuck in my own countertransference.

LINDA: I can't even remember what we talked about on Friday, let alone last Tuesday.

ALAN: [exasperatedly] Well, I don't remember where we finished up, but I remember that we were arguing all the way home.

The cutting edges of their voices make it difficult for me to listen to them, let alone comprehend what they're saying.

LINDA: Well, I don't remember crying on the way home or yelling and screaming.

ALAN: [moving back in

his seat] No, but if
we spend an hour
here and I don't buy
into what you are
saying, what's the
point of continuing
it?

LINDA: Because I felt it
was something that
had to be continued.
What I'm trying to
say is that I
always . . .

ALAN: [interrupting]
This is not what we
were talking about.

They go on and on at
each other. She doesn't
listen and he never
validates or addresses
her needs. Their styles
of thinking are as
different as their dress.
He's in a pinstripe suit
and she's in jeans.

LINDA: . . . that we
are only bringing up
our problems in the
office.

ALAN: It has nothing to
do with what we
were talking about.
It has to do with
your wanting to be
heard.

LINDA: [firmly] I don't
know if that's true.
Yeah, maybe I want
to be heard. I mean
I get very angry and
I take it very
personally when
you just totally block
me out.

Linda had been in individual treatment for six months and decided to discontinue. She said the expense and focus on herself didn't help her with her marriage. She views Alan as the most important part of her life. She doesn't want to be separate from him and experiences his demand for space and his acknowledgment of differences as rejection.

ALAN: Why, because I disagree with what you are saying?

THERAPIST: [turning to Linda] Let me try to see if I can clear this up. When have you felt so unheard before this?

I think I'm becoming more open to exploring Linda's intrapsychic issues. Perhaps I haven't yet relinquished the role of her therapist at times. I feel driven to help her get a clearer picture — it's somewhat of a rescue fantasy. I couldn't rescue my mother, but perhaps I can make up for that by rescuing her. My mother was very much the child in her relationship with my father, while he was always the frustrated father in response to her.

LINDA: Only with my father.

Linda has many hostile feelings toward her father related to his tyrannical nature. He wasn't overtly or verbally abusive, Linda claims, but everyone in the house obeyed his commands.

THERAPIST: [gesturing to the empty chair]

Switch over here. I want you to reverse roles. Pretend that you are your father talking to you about this.

LINDA: About how this session is?

THERAPIST: Yes. Your father has been here listening to the way you're talking to your husband and he's telling you how he feels.

LINDA: [getting up and settling in another chair] I don't know if I can do it.

Let's see if I can break this bind. Perhaps if she sees how she responds to Alan as her father something will change. Then perhaps I can get him to empathize with her situation.

I regret not warming her up more to the scene. I get so frustrated with this couple at times that I just want to get it over with, detach. I need to change my warm-up to them. Linda is uncomfortable since she's doing a scene in front of Alan. Certainly it needed a longer warm-up and so do I. Instead of feeling spontaneous, my anxiety is pushing me.

Bill, Linda's father, is of first generation Polish descent. He has a practical, controlling style, believing that men are masters of their homes. An unskilled factory worker, he spends his free time fishing. He is a diabetic, recently had one of his legs amputated, and wears a prosthesis. Linda's mother waits on his every need. She never speaks up to him, but gets herself another beer instead.

THERAPIST: Well, try it. You'll never know until you try it.

I could have been more nurturing to her because I can identify with her. My father was the strong one, wanting to be waited on. I could have said, "I'll help you."

LINDA: Well, I guess I can try.

THERAPIST: [turning to Linda as Bill] I forget your name.

I hope I can warm her up to the role. I have a sense of her father, but I don't want to double because I may be off balance.

This was an unwise decision. If I had doubled her incorrectly, she would have corrected me. She needed me to identify with her. I needed to double her warm-up— to get into the role. I needed to be a catalyst for her spontaneity.

LINDA: Bill.

THERAPIST: [addressing Linda as her father] Oh, Bill. That's right. So, Bill, you've been here listening to Linda and Alan. They've talked and Linda is here saying she doesn't feel as if she is heard and that the only time that Alan wants to discuss anything is right here in the office. What's your opinion?

LINDA: I can't. I can't picture my father in this setting.

I didn't set the scene sufficiently. I didn't warm Linda up

enough . . . no wonder she's having difficulty. The warm-up is a very important aspect to starting psychodrama, as important as the enactment. The enactment really can't take place unless there has been a warm-up. Again, I'm being hard on her, as hard on her as I would be on myself. In many ways I've taken my father's role. It is the woman who is deficient and needs to change and isn't trying hard enough. From this standpoint, we (Linda and I) are supposed to be good girls, trying harder and straightening out all situations.

Linda's father is a simple man who does not believe in women's liberation or personal development, or the need for therapy. Linda has told neither of her parents that she is in therapy.

THERAPIST: Well, picture him talking to you frankly. If you can't do that scene, how about this? How about warming up to being your father in response to your not having listened?

I'm too detached. I'm not moving into the scene with her. If I had doubled myself, I could have been doubling her. Both of our resistances went unaddressed.

LINDA: [as Bill addressing Linda's empty chair loudly] I don't want you going on about that, that's all there is to it. There won't be boys here and I don't like the boys that you're going out with and that's all there is to it. You're not going!

Linda's mother, also a factory worker, worked the night shift. Therefore, Linda's father managed most of the parenting roles while her mother, for the most part, remained a withdrawn child, a closet alcoholic. Linda doesn't remember her mother even shopping for clothes with her.

THERAPIST: [pointing to Linda's empty chair] Now, reverse roles as Linda. How do you want to answer?

LINDA: Well, why can't I go? Why? I'm not going to be doing anything wrong. That's her boyfriend, it's not my boyfriend. I'm just gonna be there with her.

Again I've detached myself. My unconscious rage at my own father paralyzes me. I remained outside the scene. I can't conceive of doubling if I keep myself removed. As a child, I used to detach unconsciously when I was overly frightened of my mother.

It's painful for me to observe how detached from the situation I am.

THERAPIST: [looking at Linda and pointing to the empty chair] Reverse roles and answer as your father.

LINDA: [as her father] I don't care. It's not that I don't trust you. It's just that I don't want you being there. [turning to therapist] It's really halfhearted.

It's halfhearted because she's not warmed up to the role. I needed to keep her longer in her own role and double her in that role, thereby enabling her to express her anger at her father. My distancing indicates to me that I wasn't warmed up to the scene, either. I couldn't help her because I hadn't warmed up to my anger at my own father, and I need to look at that. At this point, I really feel frustrated. I can't see her clearly, and I'm unable to role reverse with him. Her inability to really express her anger at her father is in ways a mirror image for me. I could have doubled my fear of my own father, but to risk losing my cool and losing my position as therapist/director was too scary. I need to use my spontaneity and have faith in the process. The feelings in a marital session are double, twice as intense. I need to give myself time to become confident with the identity and find ways to maintain my

THERAPIST: It is halfhearted, and half hearted is how you would like to think of him. Reverse roles.

Why is she so warmed up to projecting her feelings about her father onto her husband? And given the opportunity to speak directly to the man she's really angry at, her father, she's too frightened to risk it.

spontaneity. As my fear and anxiety lessen, my detachment will decrease.

Linda prefers to focus only on herself and is resistant to working on her family of origin issues. Her sense of loyalty blinds her. Her father in some ways cared for her more than anyone else, so to speak up to him is not only disrespectful but unappreciative. At times she has been resistant to coming for treatment and has threatened Alan that she will stop.

LINDA: I don't understand why I can't go. I'm not going to do anything wrong. That's it. That's all there is to it. It's the gospel. And it doesn't matter what I'm feeling or what I'm thinking or if it is important to me. All that matters is your opinion and what you say. Because you're the father, you're the king of your castle, and I'm just living here, I guess.

THERAPIST: Alan, I'm wondering what would you want to say to him?

Joyce, you assume Alan is going double for Linda to her father. She does need a double. But by giving him an auxiliary position, I helped him identify with the male role, the role Linda is angry at. I didn't need him to warm up more to the male issue here. However, he is doing exactly what I am role modeling for him— distancing him from identifying with the anger at a father role. He has a lot of rage at his own father, who used to beat him. He knows how to detach as well as I do, even more so. So he identified with the aggressor just like I did. If I was, say, to stop the action of the role reversal I should have had Alan derole, then explore his own feelings, and I should encourage him to empathize with his wife.

Linda's parents are from a different socioeconomic class than Alan's. Alan's parents are socially involved in upper-middle-class functions, church, dinner parties. Linda's parents are retired. They live by the water and fish—a very simple life.

ALAN: You may still have decided not to

I can't believe he is responding that way.

Again, I avoided stopping him and

go along with whatever you're talking about, but you should listen to all of the reasons.

His wife just got scolded by her father and he is sticking up for him. No wonder they have trouble.

saying, for example, "Alan, you know how it is to be humiliated by a father." Linda needs to hear something like, "I know how difficult it is to speak up to an angry parent. I know how difficult it is to love yourself when you father humiliates you."

LINDA: [turning to Alan emotionally] I'm feeling very angry.

ALAN: [turning to therapist] I don't think he didn't give her the time. I mean, that's his manner.

LINDA: [turning to therapist] What I said to him, I could very easily have said to Alan.

ALAN: You just said that to me. I just sat here saying you might as well be talking to me.

This is not the way I expected him to respond. I feel like I've made matters worse by suggesting the enactment.

I can see now that he is following my lead, my detachment.

THERAPIST: What do you mean, you are angry?

I need to figure out what to do. Issues move so quickly, it is hard at times to keep up with them.

ALAN: [surprised] You're angry at me?

LINDA: I feel the same way in response to him.

Now she's angry at her husband, when my intention was to have her direct it at her father.

ALAN: [exasperatedly] When was the last time that I said, "No, I don't want to hear about it."

I'm not sure how to let this man know he's rejected Linda just like her father did.

Well, I can see now that if I allowed myself to experience my feelings I could have doubled for Linda. However, there are so many strong feelings emerging, I lose any possibility of feeling spontaneous.

LINDA: Well, you say, "Because I said so." You just said it two weeks ago when we were going home.

ALAN: Yeah, it gets to the point where we're going round and round and round and I say, all right, we are not going to talk about it anymore because we're not getting anywhere.

They're off and running again and I don't even feel like stopping them.

LINDA: It seems to be an order.

ALAN: No, it's not an order. I'm disengaging from something that's fruitless.

LINDA: Well, I take it as an order. I mean . . .

ALAN: [interrupting] I'm not giving you an order. [louder and harsher in tone] All I'm saying is I'm not doing it anymore. I'm not going to listen anymore.

It is obvious to me that Alan has a lot of anger that needs to be worked out. I've suggested that he join group therapy. He's been reluctant to do that and the setting here is not appropriate. I need to be more direct with him. I need to tell

		him that he needs to find some place to work on his rage. This is not an appropriate place. Personally, I find his anger somewhat frightening, so I'm sure that Linda must be feeling similarly and I need to address that. Again, he knows how frightened he was of his father's rage. All three of us have had angry, rageful fathers. I could share some of my experience and serve as a role model.
LINDA: You say, "I don't want to hear it." [voice heightened and more emotional] It's more like, "Shut your mouth, I don't want to hear it."		
ALAN: I wish you would stop going on and on and on. We're not getting anywhere. [sharper in tone and punctuating his words] And you won't do that. You have to keep talking and talking and pushing me into a corner, trying to get me to do I don't know what.	This is ridiculous. I need to I stop this. I wish I could just say, "Stop."	Well, it appears to me now that did stop inside, I detached.
THERAPIST: Wait, I'm a little confused.	I'm reluctant to put pressure on Alan. He	It appears he is taking the role of his father and

Linda, can you see how you feel the same way towards Alan as you did towards your father?

has been so stressed lately.

speaking as angrily to Linda (and I guess at times to his children) as his father spoke to him. I need to put him in the role of his wife and reverse roles so that he can get an idea of how he is doing this. This just doesn't seem the appropriate setting. I don't seem to be able to warm him up in here to do that. I'm reluctant to ask him to do that, not being sure how Linda will react and whether she will support him. I'm also fearful of his anger, as I was of my father's, and get stuck in wanting to be good, which takes away my spontaneity. It feels as if I can't get it right, I can't do anything.

LINDA: Yeah. That's what I said.

THERAPIST: Okay. And can you see how it is a different role? I mean in one role you're a child responding to your father.

LINDA: Sure. But [gesturing to Alan] I would feel more angry towards him because I should have just as much of a right and opinion as he does.

ALAN: [interrupting]
    Why do I have to
    adopt your beliefs?

Alan follows the same profession (banking) and has the same
position as his father, vice president of commercial lending. Alan
recently was fired after five years of service and is establishing a
consultant firm with a financial group who were previously his
customers. His stress level recently due to the job loss has
increased considerably.

LINDA: I'm not saying
    that you do.
THERAPIST: As Alan, it
    sounds to me as if
    you're saying, "If I
    don't listen and
    agree with you, then
    you feel I haven't
    listened to you."
    Unless he adopts
    your beliefs, he is
    saying, you feel he
    hasn't listened.

That was good, Joyce.
This is what this couple
continually needs, a
person to double them
to each other, stimulate
more validation, apply
focusing techniques,
concretize their feelings,
and clarify the
information each is
sending to the other.
That is the most that
can be done right now.
I can't move this couple
to a place where they are
not developmentally
ready to be, nor do I have
a right to do that. I can't
rescue or fix them. I can
only be there with them!

LINDA: I'm not saying
    that!
ALAN: [raising his voice]
    No, I'm saying that.
LINDA: [looking at the
    therapist] I'm
    confused.

THERAPIST: [looking at Linda] It sounds as if, if he doesn't adopt your beliefs, you don't feel listened to.

Now, that was a direct statement that she could agree with or not. "How come you are not as direct with him?" Again, it's my fear of his anger. I need to reassure myself that I can manage it and he can manage it. I am much more critical of Linda as a woman than I am of Alan as a man. I have greater expectations of Alan than I do of Linda. They need to be equal. As a matter of fact, I need to diminish my expectations. This is their marriage, not mine. I need to examine my own transferential issues here. It definitely seems as if Alan becomes my father and I become the good child.

LINDA: I don't think it's true.

ALAN: Oh no! We spent more than an hour and a half last Friday and now 20 minutes or so talking about the same thing in this session.

LINDA: But there's no change. I mean after we spent all that time the last session

discussing his
smoking, can't we
compromise? Do we
all have to be
inconvenienced by
his smoking? Why
can't he be
inconvenienced by
it?

Alan had tried to stop smoking several times in the last three months. He told his children he would stop. With the job loss and challenges of trying to find a job, or possibly a business venture with some colleagues, he has been under a great deal of stress and smoking more than ever.

LINDA: And personally, I could be wrong, but I think he was even a little surprised in the session last week when you said, "Well, Alan, would you be willing to go into the bathroom to smoke?" and he said "No." There was no compromise.

Wait, I can't remember what happened two weeks ago. What am I now, the disciplinarian? This is difficult. I would have trouble with this smoking myself.

THERAPIST: After that statement, didn't it turn around? Wasn't there a discussion that led to a compromise?

Could she be correct? Maybe I neglected to complete the issue. I can't remember. Things get so confused.

It is understandable that I get swept away by this couple. It is my responsibility to remember what took place. However, in my individual and group work, I'm usually able to recall past events with ease. So I'm concerned about not having the same recall in these sessions. However, these sessions are stressful. There is twice as much material to keep track of and the stress level adds to my own sense of inadequacy. I had to remind myself that this is their marriage. I'm only the therapist here to facilitate the process.

ALAN: I think so.

LINDA: You just said you wouldn't be willing to compromise. I mean, Alan, you said "No." And that was it. And I feel as though . . .

ALAN: [interrupting] It doesn't work with you.

What is he saying? This dialogue is hard to follow.

THERAPIST: What? Compromising doesn't work?

ALAN: Yeah.

LINDA: I don't . . .

ALAN: [interrupting] I've tried that. It doesn't work.

Well, who does he think he is? What is he doing here if he isn't willing to compromise?

LINDA: It doesn't work because you're not willing to inconvenience yourself. Not that compromise doesn't work.

Whenever Alan gets depressed, Linda gets anxious and argues more and more with him. Although I've discussed this with her, she seems seduced every time. Her mother is a very depressed, withdrawn person who was unavailable to Linda all through her childhood.

THERAPIST: [turning to Alan] If compromise is not going to work, how are you going to mend this marriage? Both of you have to compromise. I mean . . .

I could double for Linda and say, "It is very difficult to see you depressed. My mother has been depressed my whole life."

LINDA: [interrupting] I feel as though . . .

THERAPIST: [interrupting] This is not one of those made-in-heaven relationships, you know, that works easily. I'm asking both of you, what will work?

I'm so frustrated. I don't feel like doubling either of them.

ALAN: [angrily to the therapist] Well, I don't think she has any right to ask me until she can understand where I'm coming from. And she hasn't even tried to do that.

I'm getting angry; I'd better summarize what he said so I know I heard him correctly.

In reflection, I can see that one thing I can do is address how frustrated we all are, and how I had stated this initially at the beginning of the session, and here we are again, each wanting the other to understand and neither being able to empathize with the other.

THERAPIST: So you don't feel that she has . . .

ALAN: [interrupting] I've tried to equate it to her eating [referring

to her diabetes], her
weight, any number
of . . .

LINDA: [angrily] How do
you know that I don't
equate it to my
eating?

ALAN: [shaking his head]
Well, obviously, you
have absolutely no
conception of . . .

LINDA: No, I can't see
the similarity. I'm
willing when you're
feeling tense to
massage your
shoulders, to scratch
your back, the kids
will even scratch
your back, they'll do
anything when you're
feeling tense so that
you don't have to
have a cigarette. I
told you that I won't
buy you cigarettes.
I'll hide the ashtrays,
I'll do whatever I
have to do. Nobody
has ever said that to
me about anything.
[Linda's diabetic
disease was ignored
in her adolescence by
her parents.]

Again, I could have
doubled Linda in her
desperate desire to take
care, feel cared for, not
lose her husband. She
lost her mother to
drinking, and nearly lost
herself to diabetes.
However, the issue of
control she is expressing
is something I struggle
with also. It feels too
close to home and not
something I'm clear
about. So it isn't
surprising that I let the
moment pass.

Linda, until she entered therapy, had given Alan responsibility
for caring for her diabetes. He gave her the insulin injections daily,
although he found it overwhelming. During the last nine months,
Linda, although she still doesn't watch her diet, has taken respon-

sibility for testing her urine and giving herself the required daily insulin dosage.

ALAN: That's
    meaningless. That's
    why I'm saying to
    you . . .
LINDA: Go ahead. Why
    is it meaningless?
ALAN: [loudly] Because   Gosh! Is he arrogant!   I can see how Linda
    it's meaningless. It   has put herself in a
    doesn't offer me   position of shaming
    anything.   him into this continued
                                                         smoking. She has
                                                         difficulty empathizing
                                                         with him. It's
                                                         understandable that
                                                         she's not going to have
                                                         empathy for cigarette
                                                         smoking, but I needed
                                                         to double him more. I
                                                         need sometimes to stop
                                                         the action and just
                                                         double one because
                                                         when they go at each
                                                         other, I get stuck in the
                                                         middle, a place I got
                                                         stuck in with my own
                                                         parents, a very
                                                         uncomfortable place.

LINDA: Isn't it a type of
    support?
ALAN: No!
LINDA: Isn't it helping
    you?
ALAN: [even louder]
    No! It's meaningless.

LINDA: It's just as if we went to the store and . . .

I'd like to let them go on in this cat-and-dog fight and just remove myself.

ALAN: [interrupting] All right, stop it. There's nothing you can do to help me stop smoking.

THERAPIST: All right. But what you're also saying, if I hear you correctly, is that you don't feel she is able to empathize with you.

ALAN: [emphatically] Right.

He sounds as if he's really getting angry—maybe I should intervene. It's hard to find the opportunity.

THERAPIST: Then could you reverse roles and show her what you would require of her to do that?

It is a good idea to move to some action here. However, asking Alan to reverse into a role he has a lot of anger with right now is rather difficult. Yes, she does need some role training. However, it might have been wise for you to take Alan's role and do some role training for him and then let him try to take the role. By asking him to do something that he still feels inadequate to do only increased his incompetence in the role.

ALAN: [shrugging his shoulders] I don't know.

THERAPIST: You're the only one who can tell her what you need. How can she help you?

The leftover debris from the extramarital relationship lurks in this couple's relationship. Alan always seems to feel he is going to be attacked for something.

ALAN: Well . . .

LINDA: [interrupting] It requires a . . .

ALAN: [interrupting] Something that is positive and reinforcing. I might as well leave it alone and not say anything.

This passive stand by Alan has been the way he has maintained himself in the marriage since the extramarital relationship. "We'll just leave things alone and they'll be okay." He doesn't know how to express his needs, and if I could release myself from transference here, I could possibly just double his needs to her, offer him role training, and give her an idea of what he needs.

He seems so shy, so reticent. He seems to wither when she speaks, and fade—I wish she would stop. He left the marriage once to regain his sense of worth from another woman. He could act out easily—she seems to always push him to repeat it.

THERAPIST: I understand that. But what I'm suggesting is that from an ideal standpoint, could you take the role and give her an idea of how you would like her to be?

ALAN: Ideally, I'd like her to stay silent.

THERAPIST: Silent?

I didn't expect him to respond this way—the least he could do is show her what he wants.

ALAN: I mean I wouldn't mind if periodically, she said, "I wish you would stop smoking. I really care about you and I want you to stop smoking, and . . ."

LINDA: [interrupting] But I do.

ALAN: [loudly] Don't nag me about it. Don't offer me meaningless suggestions like, "I'll lose weight if you stop smoking," because it doesn't work. Or "If you love me, you would stop smoking."

Okay, at least he is speaking up. Perhaps I can get him to go deeper.

This is a good place for me to double him, double his anger. I'm keeping my distance from him. I need to double his anger, and let it hang out, and then move into action when he realizes that it's anger toward one of his parents. I seem reluctant to get near his anger. I'm sure it reminds me of my father being angry at me for not doing everything the way he would want it.

THERAPIST: So, if I hear you correctly, you're saying you just feel she's on your case about smoking, and that makes you defensive.

ALAN: Yeah.

THERAPIST: And how does that relate to your life?

ALAN: She's saying, "You don't love me because you're not like me."

LINDA: I've never said that.

THERAPIST: Yeah, but the feeling of someone always on your case reminds me of your father. Doesn't Linda become in some ways like your father who was punishing you all the time? Doesn't this warm you up to your old feelings that he is just out to get you?

ALAN: I guess so. There is nowhere I can go to get away.

THERAPIST: Well, wasn't that true with your father too? And in some ways, Linda,

becomes your
father. I mean
similar to . . .

ALAN: I guess so. . . .   I'd like to get him to
I mean he was   enact a scene, but he is
always after me. It   so rigid, so concerned
wasn't like I did   about his image. I'd like
anything. If she   to believe I can warm
really understood   him up to it. Let me try.
what it was like for
me, then she
wouldn't be doing
this.

THERAPIST: Could you
show us what your
father was like?
Could you show her
so she understands?

LINDA: I think it has
nothing to do with
his stopping
smoking.

THERAPIST: Oh.   Every time I try to
intervene in this session,
one of them refuses. I
feel so blocked.

ALAN: Like I said, there   I allowed their
is absolutely nothing   dialogue . . . Linda
she or anybody else   was making an attempt
can do to make me   to help me and instead
stop smoking. It is   I felt as if I was cut off
something I have to   from getting into the
do.   scene and that she
didn't want to see the
scene that he would
have with his parents.
And his concrete
response back to the
idea of smoking gives
me the sense that
neither Linda nor Alan

want to get into a scene with Alan talking to his father. I stay away from my anger at my father. He stays away from his anger at his father. Linda stays away from her anger at her father. All three of us seem to be in some silent pack. We will not address our fathers.

During his adolescence, Alan spent time in a residential treatment center for drug addiction. In many ways he challenges, "acting out" in response to authority. The "nobody can make me" attitude seems to pervade. His extramarital relationship for nine months, some three years ago, appears to have been such an acting out. At times I'm reluctant to place stress on him and reactivate his deviant nature.

THERAPIST: And this sounds like your father saying that you've got to do this, you got to do that, almost breaking you, punishing you until you would say "Okay." Now instead, you're saying, "No, I'm not doing what you're asking me to do."

ALAN: [tiredly] I tried saying no to my father.

Joyce, you need to help him warm up to taking his father's role.

THERAPIST: And what happened?

ALAN: I had to give in. I
remember one
occasion. I don't
know what he
wanted from me. He
asked me a question
and I said no and he
beat me, asked the
question again and
again, I said no and
he just continued to
beat me until I
eventually said yes.
He'd say, "Yes what?"
Then I'd have to
reply, "Yes, Dad."

Alan's parents, both Dutch, attend church four times a week as
they did during Alan's years growing up. His mother keeps an
immaculate home and entertains guests as required. She never
tried to stop her husband from beating Alan, which according to
Alan occurred almost nightly.

LINDA: [angrily] If he
treated you like a
human being,
maybe we wouldn't
be having this
difficulty.
THERAPIST: [turning to
her] Does that help
you understand
Alan's difficulty in
responding to your
emphasis on his
need to quit
smoking?
LINDA: Well, as he was   Here we're analyzing
relating the story, it   the scene, I'm enabling

made me think
maybe it's not just a
matter of principle
because somebody
wants him to do
something. Maybe
he now feels, "I have
the power. I didn't
have the power
before, my father
did, but now I have
the power and even
if I want to or even
try to stop smoking,
I don't have to do it,
and I'm not going to
do it."

ALAN: I don't know if
it's that. But if I
don't want to do
something and
somebody pushes
me to do it, the
harder they push,
the more I resist. It's
almost unconscious.
I'm totally resistant
when it comes to
smoking. I don't
want to hear about
it. When I'm ready
to stop, I'll stop.

Well, at least he's aware
of how resistant he can
be.

her to analyze a scene.
We haven't moved into
action yet. Moving
them into action is so
difficult. I feel so stuck.

I'm aware that when he
refuses to do something,
that's it! And I feel he's
not warmed up to
enacting this scene
with his father and I
need to double the
resistance. I'm not
doubling the resistance.
I'm running from it as if
I'm asking something
that doesn't need to be,
that they're going to
refuse. I need to double
his resistance. Say,
"Okay, I don't really
want to show this to
you. I'm not sure how
you will act if you see
my relationship with
my father. You may
ridicule me, you may
shame me. It is
frightening to let you

see it, it is frightening to be here with a woman seeing it again as my mother saw it and have neither one of you do anything." Instead of doing that, I help. them move back into a discussion about the smoking. I move away from the action.

Alan had moved out when he had an affair, saying he wanted out of the marriage. After four months, during which Linda was beside herself with pain and anxiety, he returned, saying he realized he had made a mistake. It was just a fling.

THERAPIST: Outside of not talking about smoking, when you're talking about other things, are the two of you actually getting along better? Are both of you saying that you don't argue as much, fight as much? Or that you don't talk about it at all?

ALAN: Well, we still argue. It used to be that if we had an argument on Thursday, it would last until next Tuesday.

THERAPIST: I recall that. Both of you came in angry, having not

I started this session by saying I didn't know what we were

talked to each other for most of the previous week. So what you're saying is that arguments don't last as long anymore.

accomplishing here, that I felt that neither one wanted to work, and now I'm helping them agree that they've moved into a position where they argue less. I need to confront them with what's next or else they'll do nothing and remain at status quo.

ALAN: Last Thursday night we had an argument, and it was a little strained Friday morning.

THERAPIST: How is it different for you, Linda?

Maybe this work is progressing more than I believed. Perhaps outside the sessions their behavior has improved more than I'm aware.

LINDA: I can see the change in me. I mean, I start over, or it's not as important as maybe I would have thought at an earlier time.

ALAN: That's one thing I've noticed. If I had a hard day and snapped, that was it for the night. Now it kind of blows over. I think that when we're talking about this specific problem . . .

THERAPIST: [clarifying] Smoking?

ALAN: No, the problem of having fights last for a long period of time.

THERAPIST: Oh, okay.

ALAN: There wouldn't necessarily be any change in me. I mean, I was more or less the same on the topic of smoking, but there are other issues where there has been a change.

THERAPIST: I see.

ALAN: In this particular issue, I mean I'm not the one who stayed mad for five days.

They're moving again into the role of being siblings with mother and I am moving right into it with them. If I move them into action and change the sociometry, perhaps a change in this relationship will take place.

LINDA: That's not true. I mean you wouldn't talk.

ALAN: [loudly] Because you weren't talking.

LINDA: You made no effort to resolve it, but many a time I would say, "Okay, how about we start all over and not ruin the whole weekend?"

I need to point out to them that they're now looking at the past. It was good to look back to see what they gained. They need to stop arguing now about who did what in the past and look at the present. They need to move forward. They can look back, but they need to focus on the present. I need to ask each to tell the other how each perceives change. I need to say, "Alan, could you tell Linda some of the ways in which you've seen her change?" Linda could tell Alan some of the ways in which he has changed. Only then will they be able to support each other.

ALAN: Right. I would stay away from you until you were ready.

THERAPIST: I hear you saying that Linda is changing.

It is so hard to get him to give her any strokes.

ALAN: I think that we are able to disengage from arguments, which we were not able to do before.

THERAPIST: And you're saying, Linda, that you see the same improvement.

LINDA: I see myself. It's funny that he can see me, but he can't see himself. I can see myself. I know what I'm doing. I know what I'm saying.

Linda makes an important point here. Alan has difficulty perceiving himself. Even when he's watched the tapes he's been surprised at his own mannerisms. He has no sense of his mirror image, while Linda does. He needs more reflection and I need to provide that through action work. I need to in some ways use the confrontive mirror technique with him and I've been reluctant and timid.

THERAPIST: Do you see an improvement?

LINDA: Yes. I know I step back and let things slide or try to understand what he's going through. I don't see that much of a change in him, though there are times when I notice him doing something sweet that he normally didn't do. Off the top of my head I just can't think of what it was, but I just feel that a lot of difference comes from me. Maybe I was the cause of it all. By my changing the way I react, it changes the whole thing. I don't know, but I see what I do.

ALAN: I think in most cases we're able to disengage before it gets to the point

It's sad that she thinks change is all up to her—I don't know what to say.

where I'm not
listening anymore.
THERAPIST: Perhaps in
the past you would
act out in some way.

I'd like to say to Alan,
"Like when you had the
affair?" but he might
become scared of being
visible and withdraw, so
I'd better hold off.

Joyce, perhaps he won't
run so quickly from
being seen. Perhaps he
doesn't need to hide so
much. You need to test
it. You may be right that
his affair was acting
out, but you need to
test it now. You need to
test his need to hide.

ALAN: Before I would
lose my temper.
Now it's easier. Like
the other day, she
was out when I got
home from work so I
fell asleep on the
couch. As soon as
she walked through
the door, she started
yelling at me, "Why
can't you entertain
my son for an hour?"
She went on with
this, that, and the
other thing. I blew
up and said, "Why
don't you just go
back where you
came from. What
brought this on?
Why this attitude?
Just go back where
you came from."
THERAPIST: So you see
that as being less
angry?

That doesn't sound very
understanding to
me—I'm glad you're
not married to me.

Now is the time to ask
about some sociometry.
For example, say to
Alan, "So when Linda
said that, whom did she

remind you of?" He needs to get in touch with the transferential issues that are coming up in relationship to Linda.

ALAN: I was angry. Yeah.

THERAPIST: How did it end?

LINDA: I went to the A&P and after that I went to the . . .

ALAN: [interrupting] And then you went to the Board of Education meeting.

I've been conned right back into listening to their lives and they again are not interacting with each other and not taking responsibility for their relationship.

THERAPIST: What happened after that?

This sounds like existing, not living. What a marriage!

ALAN: What happened was, I went to bed at 9:30.

LINDA: [turning to the therapist] I feel lately that our lives are very boring. He's always tired, and with all the rain he hasn't done anything outside. He has absolutely no ambition to do anything inside the house either. So, I've been painting our bedroom for months,

taking wallpaper
down and everything.
I got him to help me
one day with it, but
it's like the first
paycheck he gets,
"I'm gonna hire
somebody to do
it . . . or I'm gonna
end up doing it and
it's not going to be a
good job because
I'm not good at it."
But during the week,
I don't even bother
asking him to help
because he won't do
it, and then on the
weekends lately, you
know, he just hangs
around and doesn't
do anything. So I
just feel we're
constantly hanging
around and . . .

Well, this is an improvement. In the past when Alan would get depressed and read more, or just withdraw, probably a different style but similar to Linda's mother's withdrawal, Linda would fight with him. That emotional initiation on Linda's part seemed to give some aliveness or stimulation to Alan, who at least then reacted, and that seemed like a better or easier state for him and Linda to function within.

ALAN: [interrupting]
Your expectations of
what we should do
are different from
mine. I . . .

LINDA: [interrupting] Isn't this back to where we started, compromise? I thought in the beginning that if I wanted the bedroom done it should be my responsibility, because it's more important to me to get it done.

THERAPIST: Couldn't you jointly plan these types of jobs?

ALAN: I'm not talking about the bedroom, I'm talking about weekends in general. I'm sitting in the kitchen reading and drinking my coffee and you're with the kids, telling them, "Clean your room, clean the bathroom." You're cleaning this, you're cleaning that, you want the bedroom done, you want this done, you want that done. I feel like here I am home from work and it's like I have another job with another boss and another set of things that have to be done and . . .

They're starting up again. Maybe I can stop the circular spiral before they get too warmed up. Let me see if I can get them to focus concretely on an issue and avoid another flareup.

LINDA: [interrupting] I don't ask you to do anything.

Well, at least they're having a conversation with each other. Alan is trying to explain his response to a concrete task. This is an improvement and I'm managing the situation so far.

ALAN: Why can't the house get cleaned during the week when I'm not home? I mean, why when I come home do you have to start cleaning?

LINDA: Because during the week, we are running around: here, there, and everywhere.

ALAN: During the day, I mean.

LINDA: I don't clean their bedrooms. I want them to do it.

ALAN: Yeah, but . . .

They're off again, their voice pitches are raising and the intensity and speed of their reactions have increased. They will be in another cat-and-dog fight—I don't even feel like stopping them.

LINDA: And they make a mess in the bathroom and a mess in the rec room, so I try to clean up after them, most of the time unsuccessfully.

ALAN: [interrupting] I feel like I just want to sit and do nothing. I get the feeling you disapprove because you think I should be doing something.

This man wants the house to function as if it was his office, from 9 to 5 and only on weekdays.

LINDA: Well, that's your feeling. I will usually after a while ask you, by saying something like, "I think it would be a good idea if you hang up your suits."

THERAPIST: [turning to Alan] You're living with two kids. It's unrealistic to think you could just have a peaceful, tranquil home environment.

You could have just let them go, yet it is important for them to learn how to manage each other's thoughts and feelings in response to what occurs and be able to process the situation. Joyce, you could have helped Alan process his reactions and say, "It sounds like I've heard this type of response from you before. Is this role interaction familiar? Did it exist in your home when you were a kid?" Or you could have stimulated his memory by saying, "Wow! This sounds a little bit like one of the roles in your own family!" and see if he came up with something similar.

ALAN: It's particularly bad on a really miserable day because there's nothing to do but be in the house.

LINDA: Why don't we take a ride down to the shore on Sunday? It's so peaceful on the boardwalk and we could walk along the ocean. We could let the kids get a slice of pizza. I'll drive one way, you drive the other way. If I ask you to do that, you'll reply, "I don't like driving down to the shore. That's the one thing I don't feel like doing on a weekend is going down to the shore. I don't like the beach when it's cold."

THERAPIST: So then could one of you come up with some alternative suggestion?

LINDA: Well, I would probably say, "No." Part of my point is that this is

They both have to defend their positions. It drives me nuts.

This would have been a good time to double Alan by saying, "Why should we go to the shore? All we do is argue."

something that's important to me, and something I'd like to do. I do things or go places or help him in the yard when I know damn well that I have ten loads of wash that have to be done (I'm exaggerating a little bit), but I'll help him sometimes in the yard. But I don't feel that I get anything back. You know, I do things that I don't want to do but I know they're important to him.

THERAPIST: How do you two structure your weekends? How do you decide what you're going to do? Is there a discussion?

ALAN: No. I like my weekends totally unstructured. I like everything totally unstructured. She likes everything structured. She would love it if we planned all of the meals for next week and then went to the store and just bought what we needed.

If I gave the discussion back to the two of them, we could be here all night.

Sounds like a good idea to me, but thank God this isn't my marriage.

Now is a good time to discuss with Alan his view of what some of the responsibilities of a husband and parent in a family of four. Include an exploration of structure and compromise.

THERAPIST: Well, is there an effective way you can compromise with each other?

You need to process and tell them an effective way to compromise with each other, not ask them. They don't have the skills to do it themselves.

ALAN: Yeah. There are times when we agree. That there is this or that that we want to get done.

LINDA: And that is the only time we get things done, when we plan it. I mean, whether it is going to the store or visiting somebody, we have to plan to get it done. Having an unstructured life doesn't seem to work for us because we end up doing nothing, going nowhere, and accomplishing nothing.

ALAN: That's because you and I can't agree on where to go.

LINDA: No, it's because we don't even discuss it.

Let me intervene before they start battling again.

THERAPIST: For example, when you say you can't agree on where to go, what happens?

You know what happens, Joyce, you don't need to ask them. You need to explain to them how they each

need to take some
responsibility for the
relationship and make
some effort each to
change. Develop some
problem-solving
techniques.

LINDA: I think I would
be happy going
anywhere.

ALAN: Where's
anywhere?

LINDA: Joyce just asked
you, "What do you
mean you can't
agree?" I get
frustrated when you
say we can't agree
on where to go. If
you asked, "Do you
want to go the
museum in New
York?" I'd jump at it.
If you asked, "Do
you want to take the
kids to the zoo?" I'd
jump at that, too.

ALAN: You don't jump
when I say, "Let's
take the kids to the
zoo."

LINDA: No, well . . .

ALAN: And if I said let's
go to a museum in
New York, you'd say,
"Drop me off at
Aunt Vicky's and
then you go to the
museum."

LINDA: [angrily] That's
not true.

Don't tell me we're
going off on another
tangent! They sound as
angry as when they
came in. I feel so
defeated.

ALAN: [louder] It is true. We'll probably have to stop and see Aunt Vicky while we're in New York.

LINDA: I would like to explain. When my uncle was dying, the only way I got to see him was when I got Alan to take me to New York City and take the kids to the museum.

Here we go again. I feel like Mommy here, which is not enjoyable. They each want to validate their reasons for feelings and doing what they do to me. This feels strongly like sibling rivalry.

ALAN: No, don't say that, that wasn't the only way.

LINDA: That was the only way. You weren't going to go upstairs and sit in my uncle's apartment.

ALAN: Well, we had the kids and I'm not going to park the car in that neighborhood and walk around with the kids.

THERAPIST: [seeing that Linda's eyes were filling] Could you express the feelings that are coming up for you, Linda?

Poor child, she gets so overwhelmed.

You need to double for Linda when her eyes fill up. All you needed to say is, "This is very difficult for me. I feel lost and sad. It's painful to see how little you understand me or want to please me."

LINDA: [reaching for a tissue] I don't know.

I don't know what the feeling is. I feel like he is turning something around. [hiding her head in her hands] I would have loved for him to come with me and visit my aunt or to be with my family but he never wants to bother. So I figure that I'm at least getting what I want. He's sort of getting what he wants, because he doesn't have to deal with my family, he can take the kids to the museum.

THERAPIST: Did you ask him?

LINDA: [more relaxed and back to her regular composure] I don't remember how we discussed it. But I think he made it known.

Her feelings are so brief. It is difficult to get her to hold onto them long enough for me to concretize them and expand them by doubling her. She has a quick switch.

ALAN: You said, "Why don't we do it this way?" and I said, "Fine."

LINDA: I mean, I used to love to visit all my aunts and uncles. The only way I see them now is at funerals or weddings.

I don't feel close to
any of them.

ALAN: And to me that's
torture.

THERAPIST: What's
torture?

ALAN: To go from house
to house and visit
with people that we
have absolutely
nothing in common
with and talk about
things that I know
absolutely nothing
about.

They're off and running
again—this is so tiring.

LINDA: [loudly] Well,
we do that with your
family.

ALAN: [sharply and
pointedly] And I
don't like to visit
with my family
either. I try to not go
except on Christmas
and holidays.

I need to address both
of them and say, "It's
okay to be different.
You can each be
yourself." This isn't a
contest of who turns
whom into a twin. They
have such different
types of boundaries.
Alan's are rigid and
Linda's mesh. What a
dance they do. I know
if I say that, it's going to
set Linda off into again
feeling as if she is all
alone and separate.
Since the time to end
the session is drawing
near, I'd better not
make the comment.

LINDA: [sarcastic] Well,
you're the family
man, right?

ALAN: [sharply] I don't
like to visit and sit
and talk to people!

LINDA: It's true.
[turning toward
therapist] Sunday,
we came from my
brother's house. I
mean, we got out of
there a little sooner
than I wanted, but I
figured okay, we
may have been there
long enough. We
came home and I
saw my girlfriend
with her new baby
across the street
visiting with her
mother. I said to
him, "Shirley is
going to be leaving
soon. Do you want
to go over and see
the new baby?" I
don't know if he was
just expecting to go
in, look at the baby,
then turn around
and leave or what.

ALAN: [loudly] I didn't
expect a bunch of
people there!

LINDA: Well, you saw
the cars.

ALAN: [continuing
loudly] Well, I didn't
think about it. I
knew Shirley was
visiting her mother
and I expected to

see the baby and leave.

LINDA: And that's what we did. We walked in. I was talking to Shirley and playing with the baby. He stood there and said, "There is nothing more boring than watching a baby." When they asked if we would like to stay for dessert or a cup of coffee, I just told him, "Why don't you go home—I'll stay for a while."

ALAN: That was fine. It didn't bother me.

LINDA: But you didn't have to make that kind of remark. They said they wished you could have stayed. I wanted to tell you that it was rude.

ALAN: It wasn't rude.

THERAPIST: You have difficulty with Alan leaving their home instead of staying and visiting?

What's bothering her now? There's always so much to complain about in these sessions. They both just gripe, gripe, and gripe.

I need to structure this couple and say, "Come in with one issue between you to discuss." I think that this free processing style allows Linda to jump from one statement to another, with no resolution. She just has one complaint after another. Instead of one problem being focused on in which she can finally receive some sense of satisfaction or resolution, the list of gripes grows and grows.

LINDA: I have a problem with it, but I feel that I deal with it. I'm just pointing out how very difficult it is.

ALAN: [sharply] Well, you said it was rude. To me it wasn't rude. I had no desire to go sit in a room full of strangers and make conversation with them.

THERAPIST: The two of you sure argue about everything.

LINDA: Well, what kind of world would this be if nobody sat around making conversation with anybody?

Let me interject before she gets any angrier and makes resentful remarks.

THERAPIST: [turning to Alan] I know you're not the ideal type of couple you want to be.

LINDA: [in a harsh bitter tone] I know that too. All right. So Saturday your sister has a birthday party for her daughter. I don't really want to go.

Well, I tried to interject and that seemed to leave Linda feeling more frustrated. It didn't work. I feel defeated.

ALAN: [loudly interrupting] No, no, no, no, No. That's bullshit!

LINDA: [sarcastically] Are you saying, "It's fine for me to stay home and you can just jump in the car with the kids?"

ALAN: I go to your brother Ryan's when you are invited. I don't say, "Fine, go to the birthday party alone."

LINDA: [with a sharp and bitter tone] Yeah. And so?

ALAN: [louder, more accusing] So don't tell me when you go to the birthday party, I'll go to Aunt Mary's because you . . .

LINDA: [interrupting] I'm just asking. I mean, if it's all right for me to jump into the car and go somewhere, then you don't have to go because you don't want to.

Let's see if I can clarify her message before she gets angrier and perhaps storms out. She's done that in the past. I'd like to avoid her putting herself in that position and then regretting it.

THERAPIST: What you're saying is, Linda, if I hear you, you feel like you have to do what he expects, and then he doesn't reciprocate.

LINDA: What I'm saying is I go with you to wherever, even though I may not feel comfortable or may not even like the idea of going, but I do it because I'm your wife and I belong next to you.

ALAN: [angrily] How often do we go?

LINDA: [bitterly] A hell of a lot more than we go to any of my relatives.

ALAN: Do we get invited to Ronnie's [Linda's brother] when it's his birthday? Does he have a party?

I need to point out to Linda that she and Alan have to agree on their expectations of the social roles they have for each other. Are they agreeing that they will both publicly be there for each other? It can't be an assumption.

Linda has two brothers, both favored by her mother. Her younger brother is a closeted homosexual and owns a florist shop. Linda's mother often helps out at the shop and continually brags to Linda about how creative he is and supportive of her getting out of the house. Linda resents the attention he receives from her mother and feels she is still totally neglected by her.

LINDA: No, Bill's [Linda's older brother] invited us for Christmas and you can't be bothered going all the way up there. My parents invited us down to the

shore, but you can't
be bothered driving
down to the shore.
ALAN: [loudly and
defensively] I do go
down to the shore.
LINDA: When was the
last time?
ALAN: I don't remember.
LINDA: I don't either.   I've lost my interest and
  Last summer was   energy in stopping
the last time we   them—clarifying or
were down to the   doubling it is an endless
shore.   job. They just want to
go at each other.

Both Linda and Alan have said in the past they dislike doing overnights with Linda's parents because her mother drinks heavily, leaves beer cans all around, and can be found sleeping wherever she crashes. Linda, although enraged at her mother's drinking and her father supplying cases of beer, refuses to confront either one about their problems.

ALAN: So you have a
problem with going
down to the shore
too. Don't lay it all
on my doorstep.
LINDA: But it's easier   I needed to double for
for me when you're   Linda how difficult it is
with me.   for her to be with her
parents, so that Alan
could have a sense of
how much she looks to
him for support in her
social roles, just as he
looks to her for support
in his work role.

ALAN: No. You don't
want to be always

going down to the
shore, either.

LINDA: No, I don't
always want to be
going down to the
shore. In fact,
having to go down to
the shore tomorrow
is a pain in the ass,
but the kids are
down there and I
have to go pick
them up. I think it's
good for the kids, for
whatever reason, if
it's guilt or I feel
upset or sad about
my childhood, I still
think my parents
enjoy having the
kids there.

ALAN: Fine, I don't
object to the kids
going there.

LINDA: I didn't say that
you did. I don't
know how we got
onto this one. I
guess I . . .

ALAN: [interrupting
angrily] I don't like
to go down to the
shore to your
parents.

LINDA: Well, I would
like to go down
more often for the
kids.

ALAN: We go down all
summer long.

THERAPIST: Haven't the kids been gone for a couple of days?

Let me distract them so we can end this session with some closure rather than a bang.

LINDA: [reflecting] Hmm, they left Sunday.

THERAPIST: You're going to get them tomorrow?

I am burnt out at this point. I'm not trying to do anything except just be with them. This is exhausting. This session needs to end. I need to stop and assist them in processing what has been happening, but I choose not to. It's just too tiring. I feel like I'm with my parents and I'm trying just to keep my head above water. I'll let them go on like this and just see how far they go. They are exhausting.

LINDA: Yes.

THERAPIST: So did the two of you do anything enjoyable?

ALAN: Yeah.

LINDA: Well, I didn't make dinner yesterday, so we ended up going to Fuddrucker's and Bradlees and then we came here.

THERAPIST: Is that what you thought when you said, "Yeah," Alan?

ALAN: I thought we had
one, even two, times
we enjoyed together.
Sunday, I was so tired.

THERAPIST: Your parents   Maybe if I stick with
came to pick them   the concrete, I can
up?   wind them down.

Although Linda and Alan have discussed not allowing the children to stay overnight with Linda's mother, given her drinking habits, Linda thinks her mother drinks less when the children are there and the children want to go, so they've been spending more time with her parents.

ALAN: They stayed at
Ronnie's.

LINDA: My parents
came to Ronnie's for
Easter and I asked if
it would be all right
for the kids to go
back with them.

THERAPIST: Did you
both have a more
enjoyable time
together, with the
kids gone?

LINDA: Actually, it   Good, they're calming
seemed a little more   down. Maybe I can
boring. I mean,   teach them how to stop
Sunday night to me   these battles by
was boring. I mean,   changing gears into
our Easter ended   different subject
very early.   matter.

THERAPIST: So what did
you do?

LINDA: Watched a
movie. We watch a
movie on any given
night.

THERAPIST: I hear you saying that the times you enjoy spending together are fewer.

LINDA: Today, it's probably a little bit worse. Maybe it sounds stupid, but I think it's because of all the rain we've been having. I feel as if we're cooped up in the house doing nothing. Like I said, I've been working on the bedroom. I mean my arm is killing me, I've been telling Alan that he's stronger and taller than I am, and that he could probably get this done at least twice as fast. But I'm getting it done. I took all the wallpaper down, stripped off all the backing paper, and even took a scratchy thing and removed all the glue.

ALAN: But what does that have to do with the level of emotionalism? It doesn't deal with where you're coming from. That doesn't change whether you're tired or not.

LINDA: I'm not saying tired, I'm just saying I feel cooped up.

ALAN: Even so, that creates tension and makes things worse. It doesn't change where you come from.

LINDA: I didn't say it did. I just said that's mainly why it seems worse.

ALAN: I think it's worse that I have to be in there. The fact that I'm not makes it worse. That's what the problem is.

This is exasperating. One hour is enough. How do they live their lives like this?

THERAPIST: The two of you have to realize there has to be some commitment to change.

I've finally got some air time to say something. They may be married to each other, but I don't need to be married to them.

LINDA: I've said this right along.

ALAN: Change what? I'm gonna have to change myself into somebody who can enjoy having an inane conversation with a bunch of people?

LINDA: No, I wasn't even thinking that.

ALAN: So stop poking me about it.

LINDA: Doesn't every couple do things for

I'm going to interrupt this dialogue because if

a spouse because the other one enjoys it? I don't, they'll warm up again and there will be no closure again. Linda just can't let go.

THERAPIST: [interrupting] I understand what you are saying, Linda, but it requires a willingness by each person, it has to be jointly agreed upon.

ALAN: What?

THERAPIST: I'm not speaking to either of you separately, this statement is for both of you. Each of you has to individually decide what you are willing to contribute or change in yourself that would be pleasing to the other person. I think it has to be thought out and decided individually. Not what someone else tells you what you have to do to please them. That sounds manipulative and controlling. It's not for you, Linda, to tell Alan what he has to change. It's for both of you to decide what would help the relationship and find compromises.

ALAN: But what I disagree with is that Wake up and smell the coffee. You have a real

she wants to change
something in me
because of a defect
she has. I disagree
with that totally.
THERAPIST: I think that
neither of you is
working on making
this a better
marriage. You're both
saying the marriage is
better because you're
not fighting as much.
Okay, now what are
we going to do to
make it even better?
LINDA: [emotionally] I
feel like I'm existing.
I'm waiting for . . .
ALAN: [interrupting] For
what, a miracle?

THERAPIST: Well, I've
thought about this
and I want you both
to think about it.
ALAN: My situation at
work has consumed
my energy for the
past year or more to
the extent that the
rest of my life is on
hold. And I am trying
to resolve that.

wife, not a dreamed-up
one.

Now this is the way to
go, Joyce. Give them
responsibility for this
marriage.

I hope I haven't given
her another idea she can
feel victimized about.
   No, for you to wake
up and realize that you
actually may have to do
some work in the
relationship.

At least I think he hears
me.

The banking industry has been so difficult over the last year
that Alan's position has undergone many changes. He was transferred to another branch, a half hour further away from home. His

perks (car and expense account) were terminated. His position at the bank changed to a much more stressful area of lending that he disliked. He started working longer hours—his work week increased two hours each day, along with Saturdays.

THERAPIST: Well, that may be true. But it seems to make more sense to talk about what you are each willing to give to the relationship and figure out a way to make your marriage less stressful. Stop the continued constant disagreement.

ALAN: We have a difference in philosophy. She wants to deal with the things that we do and I want to deal with the reasons for the things we do. She'll say, "What's wrong with our marriage is we should go for a walk every night before dinner."

Well, that's an interesting way to look at it—but how to put it into practice is another thing.

Here was the point where you could have said, "Yes, Alan, both of you are different and both of you need to compromise with each other and accept each other's pain and help each other, not defend against each other."

THERAPIST: Well, behavioral things will make changes for the moment, but the core changes that will have a long-lasting effect, involves changing the inside aspects of

the relationship and
then yourself.

LINDA: I don't think
going for a walk is
going to make our
marriage wonderful.
I think going for a
walk may give us the
opportunity to talk.
It's going to give us
the opportunity to
do something as a
family.

ALAN: And the way I
look at it is we're
always doing things
as a family and we
have the opportunity
to talk if we're sitting
in the kitchen, the
living room, or on
the stairs.

Alan may be harboring
feelings of resentment
for his affair with Sylvia,
and involving himself in
family matters may
reopen the wound.
Linda, on the other
hand, is fearful that
Alan really wants to
leave the relationship
again. She tries to get
him to show he is
interested in the
relationship by asking
him to complete
seemingly small tasks
and favors.

LINDA: [angrily]
Obviously. I guess
we don't talk
enough . . .

ALAN: [sharply and
louder] Well, then
talk. What I am
saying is, "Talk."
Don't try to tell me
that I have to take a
walk to talk.

LINDA: Well, it's not easy to talk when you're sitting in front of the TV or you're reading a book. I'm not comfortable talking like that.

ALAN: So then talk to me when I'm sitting down, before or after dinner.

LINDA: Before dinner, you're grouchy. After dinner, you get up and go into the living room.

ALAN: So then come in and talk.

LINDA: I just got finished telling you, I don't feel comfortable.

They can't put closure on what they say. Stop, stop, let's have some closure.

ALAN: After dinner, I'm waiting for something to happen while you're finishing up in the kitchen.

LINDA: You're sitting in the living room reading a book.

ALAN: No, I'm not. Not all the time.

THERAPIST: This is starting to sound like a king on his throne. Linda has to find just the right time and the right place.

This session needs to end.

Well, I'm pleased that you're speaking up and saying something to him. He needs to have some mirroring back, but I need to do it in a better context than this.

And he didn't fall apart at the statement. He said, "No, I'm waiting."

ALAN: No, I'm waiting.

LINDA: Well, that's just how I feel.

ALAN: I'm waiting for the gears to shift. What's gonna happen next? And nothing happens. So I read a book.

LINDA: Because you like your life unstructured.

ALAN: You want to structure my life, but that's not the answer.

THERAPIST: [turning to Alan] Why don't you say, "Linda, if you want to talk to me, after dinner is a good time."

ALAN: [defeated] But I just can't . . .

Well, I don't know what that means, but this session needs closure.

Alan is also afraid of getting intimate with Linda. This could be a repercussion from his affair. This fear is evident in his avoidance of allowing Linda to get close to him in any way, talking, going out together, and so on. He wants to build a shell around himself.

THERAPIST: You can't say it any more directly to her?

ALAN: If you need to talk to me, after dinner is a good time to talk.

Joyce, this could be an opportunity to do role training with him. He needs behavioral training. He needs a specific dialogue to get him warmed up.

LINDA: Okay, but could we do it on the steps or in the backyard?

ALAN: If it's nice out.

LINDA: It's not even that I need to talk to him. Sometimes I just like to sit and talk with him, sometimes just sit on the steps and watch the kids play.

I could have said, "Yes, I understand," to Linda. Tell them to allow themselves to be vulnerable.

ALAN: So we'll do that when it's nice out.

THERAPIST: [noticing Linda's eyes filling with tears] Could you express what you're feeling now? Are you feeling it would be nice if the two of you could just be together?

This was a time to double even though the session is almost over. You could say, "Again, it's wonderful to finally hear you ask me to say something. I just want to talk to you. I just want to connect with you. It's so difficult to connect with you." You could have doubled for her and had some form of closure. Your anger at them for their inflexibility and desire to be rescued is getting in your way.

LINDA: [nods]

ALAN: We are together.

THERAPIST: I wanted to take the extra time to just sit and talk, rather than watch the video session. I feel you both know what you're doing, now that may be crumbling the blocks in your relationship, but nothing is happening. It's not my marriage, it's your marriage.

Let me stop this before it continues. Let's see if I can wrap this session up.

During the past few weeks the second half of each session has been spent viewing the first half and then as an ending, we have been spending the last 15 minutes together reviewing their reactions to the video. They both seem to become involved with their own images, particularly Alan. Neither seems to be able to reflect on how to change the relationship, nor did they find the session spent in that way as confrontive. However, they did appear to confront each other all the more.

ALAN: I think the problem is the perspective. I feel that there is nothing wrong with my life and I would be perfectly happy if she would just stop pursuing all these ideas of change. She feels, I gather, that there is something intrinsically wrong with her life that needs fixing.

LINDA: No, I don't feel that something is wrong. I do feel that it could be better. And why settle for anything less then the best?

ALAN: Well, go ahead, just don't make my life miserable.

LINDA: I get discontented at times and I do think that it just could be better. I know it could be better.

THERAPIST: Perhaps, Alan, what you're saying is that your attitude has affected the relationship. You've been so absorbed in your work since the

I could have reminded Linda of how difficult she finds it to get warmed up, how she looks to others, particularly Alan, to warm her up. Then remind her that she needs to warm herself up and then relate to Alan and not always look to him to provide her warm-up.

I could have doubled for Alan and said, "I have enough difficulty trying to change and improve my professional life without also being expected to make my personal life better for you."

banking industry started failing that you've had little else on your mind, and Linda finds that your attitude has affected the marriage.

ALAN: Also, you know I get cabin fever in the winter. I hate the winter. I hate being stuck in the house.

I could have doubled Alan's depression, how stuck he has felt, or I could have asked Linda to double what she hears.

THERAPIST: And if you haven't had any energy left for your family, can you understand Linda's feelings and point of view?

ALAN: Energy left over? I guess I don't envision the possibilities she seems to think are out there, to be better or to be the best. Well, maybe we could do a few more things together and go out more often. [turning to Linda] Fine, let's do it. I think the real problem with my life is that you're discontented with it. I feel that the actual thing that we are talking about is not what we're talking about.

I could have doubled his discontent and Linda's discontent so they could experience the mutuality of the issue. They both could then experience and empathize with each other's response to Alan's loss.

THERAPIST: What is that?

ALAN: I think the argument we had last week was the effect of something else. [turning to Linda] We have to get past your problem before we can get to the real problem. The problem is you have to be heard, you feel you're not being listened to. That problem has to be dealt with before we can even begin to compromise because we're never going to get to the point where you're hearing anything.

THERAPIST: And on the other hand, your problem is that you feel you're being ordered around and it's difficult for you to bend.

LINDA: If I saw us both compromising, I would feel better.

ALAN: You want to take two steps instead of taking one?

THERAPIST: You're both going to have to make some changes, folks.

You need to show Alan how easy it is for him to see Linda and how difficult it is to see himself. And, for him, the way to improve, broaden, and deepen an interactive dialogue with Linda is to speak about himself and not attack her. If I point that out, maybe he can start to understand and recognize himself. Joyce, the man is so detached he will have difficulty without a lot of doubling on your part. In addition, he doesn't recognize himself, so how can he show Linda who he is—you are dreaming.

ALAN: And I think that's what I'm doing here. We have to change our individual problems. If we did that we wouldn't have any problems as a couple.

I should have told him, "Fine, you need to change these problems individually, I've asked you to join group. If you don't want to join group, see someone individually. Work on your problems individually elsewhere or let's work on them here. You've refused to do this, Alan." Joyce, you need to be firmer about getting a commitment from him to change, to move these sessions and create a deeper phase of growing.

THERAPIST: [standing up] Well, perhaps that's true. We are out of time for now. Let's continue with this next session.

THERAPIST REVIEW

In some ways it is no surprise to me that I chose this couple to illuminate my theories in this book, since Linda and Alan could have been my parents. As a child I always wished my parents would understand and express themselves to each other in a more loving, caring way. Here I am again with the same type of couple, hoping that they will make use of the AMP skills I offer them—and they do. However, they are both so needy it is hard for them to maintain the skills without my continual reinforcement—or so I think at this point.

Linda has no idea of how to express her feelings because, as a child, she had no role models who would say, "Let's go see the fireworks, and then have some ice cream." She continually whines, "You never help me." Instead, she could say, "Hey, how about doing the wallpaper today? Maybe we can get the two kids to help scrape and get some Chinese takeout for dinner."

Linda had no doubling by a parent or significant other. Because of this, she is unable to double herself. My continual reinforcement of her thoughts and feelings by assuming the double role for her as her therapist will in time enable her to double herself. In time, through my doubling her and role modeling, she will not need to complain to Alan that he is not doubling her and she will be able to say to Alan, "How do you feel about going to the zoo today? We can skip Aunt Mary."

Alan is so angry at his father. Having no separation, he has introjected his father from fear and he continues to imitate him. He has truly incorporated the feared parent. His father would beat him when he was a child for not being perfect. He would hit him until he begged for mercy and said, "I'll be good, Daddy." To save his sanity, he detached from the emotional pain and trauma of these incidents and today remains detached. He has become as unyielding as his father with a "you can't make me" attitude. He never heard his mother's voice lifted in protest, so he cannot hear his wife's voice. He cannot be flexible and bend enough to help his wife paint the bedroom or admire a baby. He equates unyielding self-righteousness with masculinity. This rigidity and "don't touch me" attitude holds him together—it's his way of surviving.

How does working with this couple affect me, as the therapist? To begin with, I always feel very needed, wanted, and even appreciated by them. I often feel like a mommy to two rivalrous children. They are eager to learn skills. However, once I show them how to implement new skills they require me to continually maintain them. I find myself continually and vigilantly making sure they do not get so angry at each other that they forget to use the skills they have learned. As participating adults, they now know how to double, role reverse, and understand the phases of warm-up, enactment, and closure. However, when they revert to earlier roles of rivalrous siblings, they become self-righteous and controlling, and playing out the chosen child is all that matters. Are they exhausting at times? Yes! Are they frustrating at times? Yes! Do I still feel a reward in educating and training them? Yes!

Key countertransferential issues that came up in the therapy sessions with this couple included specifics related to my experiences with my own parents. As a child I often received love and approval from my parents for trying to protect them. In these couple therapy sessions, I often found myself assuming the same role I had in my parents' relationship, and feeling ineffective and burdened and pulled in opposite directions. I realized the ineffectiveness I was experiencing as rescuer in this couple's relationship and began to give the couple responsibility for their own relationship. During this journey, I was reminded of Moreno's (1941) statement: "I wish that I had been born with you as one being. But then I thank God that I was born apart from you, so that I could meet you as a separate being. O God, O my God, now that I have met you and have become one with you, I wish that I would die with you, as one being" (p. 223).

COUNTERTRANSFERENCE

As can be readily seen from the therapy sessions reproduced in these chapters, the problems of countertransference are always present. Countertransference refers to the issues, feelings, or thoughts that surface in the clinician in response to working with the client. Such feelings and thoughts occur when the clinician's unconscious or unresolved issues from the past are triggered by an interaction with a client. Historical resurrections from the therapist's own unconscious forces are always a given. Moreno (1941) tells us that even the most experienced therapist can experience countertransferential issues in certain situations. This is not to say that these issues interfere with the present drama. Rather, they act as a bell ringer, a reminder that "I saw a play like this once, maybe I can help," or "My mother used to behave like that, but I. . . ." Thus the therapist's key element is spontaneity. To acquire this state of complete present-mindedness during a session requires that the clinician be constantly aware of those countertransferential issues that are just below the surface and are feeding the spontaneous response.

As therapists, we work in a highly intellectual, sometimes omniscient role. Our emphasis is on the client's narcissism. When working with a couple, we have two people's narcissism to be concerned with, along with possibilities of sibling rivalry for the therapist's attention.

PROJECTIVE IDENTIFICATION

Projective identification is a near possibility for us as therapists at any time. However, it is our responsibility to be aware of and manage our own feelings. Bion (1959) states that a great deal of what takes place between the therapist and client goes unacknowledged by both. Perhaps so, which is why I believe the therapist's psyche is his or her most prominent and useful tool of the trade, and therefore must be maintained in balance between the two worlds of illusion and reality. To start with this requires holding fast to our purpose as therapist. This purpose, from my point of view, is to facilitate the couple's transformation. This requires a specifically created role that develops the therapist's style, his or her relationship with the couple, and the demands required for continued focus on the couple's treatment. Once the therapist has aided the couple in adjusting to their need for treatment, the role as facilitator of treatment can be more specifically defined.

SIX-FOLD PROCESS OF THE COUPLES THERAPIST

As couples therapists, we are required to be aware of our own thoughts while listening to our patients. This requires paying keen attention to our own inner dialogue, which is sometimes hard to manage. This inner dialogue, our autotelic responses, is the key to understanding the treatment process. We need to be aware of and maintain a six-fold process: listening to each partner, doubling each partner, intervening when necessary, and all the while listening to our own inner dialogue. Keeping in mind that the struggle for truth when working with the couple is essential to the therapeutic process, the AMP supervisory tool serves as a method to accomplish all aspects of this procedure by externalizing the treatment process for the therapist to review. Just as we externalize each partner's inner dialogue through "doubling," we must also devise a means of doubling our own inner dialogue and doubling the interactions of the therapeutic triad. Once validated, we can review the externalized material from a reflective mirrored position and become aware of our own blind spots, illusions, or fantasies. Often there is a strong discrepancy between what we know and what we feel. As we facilitate the loss, grief, intimacy, and degrees of closeness (separation and attachment) of couples, we can recall our own personal issues in these areas and use them as tools. The AMP supervisory tool illuminates those areas for our review as clinicians.

COUNTERTRANSFERENCE AS A GUIDING TOOL

Helplessness is often an issue for our clients, and this can heighten our own deficiencies, our own inability to cope or ability to see the light. As therapists we insist that one must first seek treatment him- or herself before becoming one who treats. However, we persist in disavowing our needs as therapists, owing the fact that we also are continually in need of healing. It is my belief that our healing needs to be continuous, illuminated through supervision of varying types serving as a vehicle for our use as therapists. The functioning of our psychological, emotional, and spiritual makeup provides us with a composite of roles that need fine tuning in order to keep our skills functioning at their highest level. This fine tuning requires our stretching, seeking continuous growth and development in the personal and professional aspects of our lives. We have a responsibility as professionals to be role models, not pillars of perfection but human beings following our mission as treatment guides.

The more aware the therapist is of his or her own countertransferential issues in response to a client, the less unconscious influence those familial or personal issues will have on the therapeutic process. He or she must remain careful not to project his or her own feelings onto the client. Although considered negative or maladaptive, a countertransferential issue may serve as a useful tool if properly used. If the therapist is not fearful or anxious about his or her own feelings or thoughts, they will emerge spontaneously during the session in appropriate and helpful ways for the couple. For example, in sharing such feelings, the therapist could say, "I was feeling uncomfortable when you said . . . because it reminded me of when. . . . Does that remind you of any similar thoughts or feelings you've had?" However, to use this type of approach requires a good rapport between therapist and the couple.

CHAPTER

10

٭

The Way They Were

$\mathcal{A}$t the beginning of treatment, Linda said she had sought couples therapy to reduce confusion about her identity in relationship to her husband, Alan. She said that she felt insecure in the relationship and was unable to think about anything except Alan's extramarital affair. She worried that he might cheat on her again. Unable to relieve her relentless worry that the other woman might still be in his life, she felt relentlessly compelled to pursue keeping him, and at the same time driven to search for every imperfection in the relationship to validate her idea that he was not committed to her. Although Alan reassured her, she felt his statements were empty, which left her uncertain of his loyalty and convinced that he might seek out another woman.

Alan felt that Linda constantly held the affair over his head. He said that the estrangement had changed his perspective as to what was important to him. From this position, he claimed he was no longer the same person he had been when he had the affair and would never consider turning away from his wife and family for fulfillment again. He added that Linda's constant nagging for reassurance and her distrust frustrated him and left him feeling helpless.

HOW THEY SAW THEMSELVES

First Social Atom Review

The first social atom of this couple was done when they entered treatment. Obtaining the sociometric status reveals how each mate perceives him- or herself in his or her environment. Since the social atom is one means of viewing a person's sociometry, I decided to have each partner complete a social atom at the beginning, middle, and end of treatment, believing that the procedure would reveal any significant changes in the couple's sociometry, therefore in the couple's relationship during the course of treatment, to ascertain whether or not the couple would change their positions with regard to each other or in reference to other family members during the course of treatment.

Having an initial sociometric diagram would also offer information about how each partner relates to his/her world, who the others are in their environment, and how close or distant each partner feels toward others. This information would provide insight for our therapeutic triad.

The partners complete projective diagrams, social atoms, and role assessments. Their view of how they believe their mate perceives the world would offer information on how well the couple knows each other. Are they able to reverse roles with their mates? Does their ability to reverse roles with their mates improve over the course of treatment?

PROJECTIVE DIAGRAMS

The pretest diagram Linda drew (Figure 10–1) included ten symbols, one of which was quite large and represented herself. The symbol used to represent her husband was drawn above her. The symbols representing her children, daughter Moira and son Lee, were placed on either side of the symbol representing herself.

Figure 10–1: Linda's First Social Atom

Allan = Husband

Moira = Daughter

Lee = Son

Ron = Brother

Bill = Brother

Dad = Linda's father

Mom = Linda's mother

A's Dad = Allan's father

A's Mom = Allan's mother

Her mother and father were placed beneath her, with one brother on either side. She placed her mother-in-law and father-in-law far above at the end of the matrix.

The pretest diagram that Alan drew (Figure 10–2) has a larger number of symbols, fourteen. This matrix included his parents, three brothers and a sister, as well as Linda's parents, referred to as Mom and Dad G., and his two brothers-in-law (his wife's brothers). The symbol representing Lee, his son, the younger of two children, was placed slightly above and between the symbols used to represent himself and his wife. His daughter's symbol was placed directly above him. Several figures were equal in size to the figure that he used to represent himself. The symbol that represented his wife was clearly larger than the symbol for himself.

SECOND SOCIAL ATOM REVIEW

Midway in therapy a second social atom was completed (Figure 10–3). In this diagram, Linda drew eight figures in her atom. The symbol she used to represent Alan was right beneath and touching the symbol representing herself. The children were placed on either side of the symbol she used to depict herself, with each of her parents under either child. The symbol for the therapist was directly above her mother. A symbol to represent one friend was placed above her own, touching and significantly smaller in size.

The diagram Alan completed (Figure 10–4) representing his perception of Linda's social atom included fifteen symbols, none touching. The children were placed slightly above and to either side of the symbol for Linda. The symbol for himself was also above her. Included in his representation of Linda's social atom were symbols for her two brothers and her parents, as well as symbols for his parents, his brothers, and their wives.

The second diagram Alan drew (Figure 10–5) to represent himself had fourteen symbols. The symbol he used to represent

Figure 10–2: Alan's First Social Atom

Bill = Brother-in-law

Ron = Brother-in-law

Mom G. = Mother-in-law

Dad G. = Father-in-law

Linda = Wife

Barry = Brother

Dad = Father

Mom = Mother

Moira = Daughter

Lee (L.W.) = Son

Gerry = Brother

Cat = Sister

Cheryl = Sister-in-law

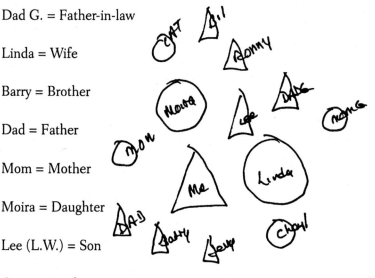

Figure 10–3: Linda's Second Social Atom

J.   = Joyce/Therapist

L.   = Friend

M.   = Daughter

L.W. = Son

Dad = Dad

Mom = Mother

A.   = Husband

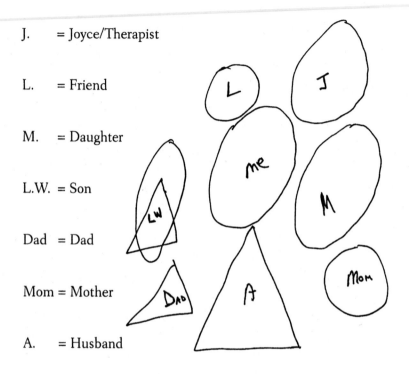

Figure 10–4:
Alan's Perception of Linda's Second Social Atom

Linda = Wife

L.W. = Son

Moira = Daughter

Mom G. = Mother

Dad G. = Father

Ronny = Brother-in-law

Bill = Brother

Mom P. = Mother-in-law

Dad P. = Father-in-law

Figure 10–5: Alan's Second Social Atom

L. = Linda

Barry = Brother

Gerry = Brother

Cat = Sister

Bill = Brother-in-law

Ronny = Brother-in-law

Moira = Daughter

L.W. = Son

Dad G. = Father-in-law

Mom G. = Mother-in-law

Mom = Mother

Dad = Father

Cheryl = Sister-in-law

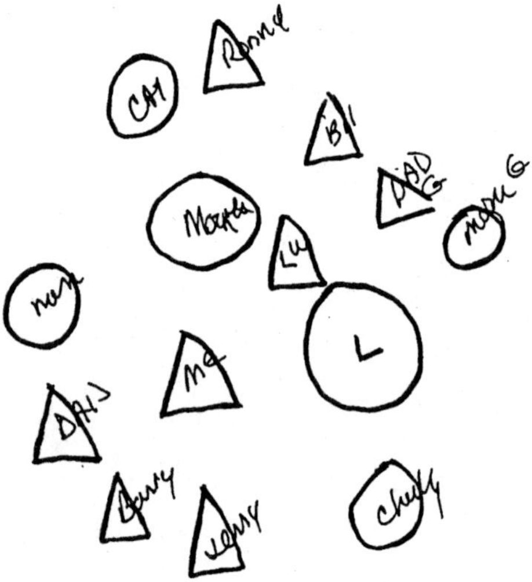

Linda was larger and to one side of the symbol he drew for himself. Both symbols representing his children, Moira and Lee, were placed above and in between his wife and himself. The symbols he used to represent his parents were to the lower left of the diagram, with the symbol representing his mother above his father. His two brothers were represented, along with his sister. The symbols representing his two brothers-in-law were of equal size at the upper segment of the diagram.

The diagram Linda completed toward the end of their therapy represented her perception of Alan's social atom and included seven symbols (Figure 10–6). The children were placed on either side of him, with the symbol for their son touching him. The symbol for his uncle (H) was over Alan, and both of Alan's parents were on the lower, outer sides of the diagram.

THIRD SOCIAL ATOM REVIEW

The last social atom completed by Linda at the end of treatment included eleven symbols (Figure 10–7). The symbol representing herself was placed in the center, while the symbol representing her husband, Alan, was above, with the children on either side of her. The symbols representing her parents and the symbols for her in-laws were facing her from the right. The symbols representing her two brothers were below her. There are no symbols placed to the left of her. One friend was included in this diagram as well.

Alan's diagram (Figure 10–8) of his perception of Linda's social atom included fifteen symbols. The symbol for himself was in the middle of the matrix, while the symbol representing Linda was facing him to his right. Below the symbol representing Linda was his mother-in-law, and below the symbol representing himself was his father-in-law. He placed his children on the left side of the symbol used to represent himself. He placed the symbols for his parents to the right, facing Linda. He included three of Linda's

Figure 10–6:
Linda's Perception of Alan's Second Social Atom

A.   = Alan

H.   = Uncle

L.W.   = Son

Moira = Daughter

L.   = Wife

D.   = Father

M.   = Mother

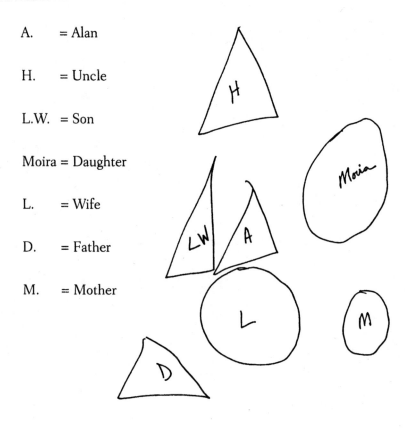

Figure 10–7: Linda's Third Social Atom

Moira = Daughter

Alan = Husband

Lee = Son

Bill = Brother

Ron = Brother

Jerry = Friend

His Mom = Mother-in-law

His Dad = Father-in-law

Mother = Mother

Father = Father

Figure 10–8:
Alan's Perception of Linda's Third Social Atom

Terri = Friend

Donna = Friend

Ceil = Friend

Bill = Brother

Ron = Brother

Moira = Daughter

Dad P. = Father-in-law

Mom P. = Mother-in-law

A.P. = Husband

L.W.P. = Son

C.P. = Sister

Barry = Brother

Dad G. = Father-in-law

Mom G. = Mother-in-law

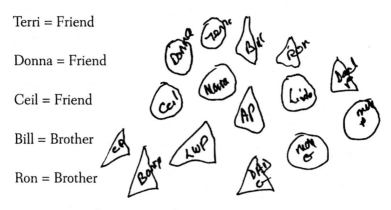

friends in the matrix and her brothers, as well as two of his brothers.

The last social atom Alan completed at the end of therapy included seventeen symbols (Figure 10–9). Alongside the symbol he used to represent himself was a symbol representing his brothers B.P. and D.P., and his sister C.P., and his sisters-in-law and brothers-in-law T.G., G.P., C., R.G., and B.G. The symbols representing his two children were on the other side of his symbol. The symbol for Linda was on the other side of the two children. Included in the diagram were other family members, sisters-in-laws, nephews, nieces, and his in-laws.

In the diagram Linda drew of her perception of Alan's social atom (Figure 10–10), she placed herself above the symbol representing Alan with the children on either side of him. Symbols representing his parents were to the right, facing him, and the symbols for her parents were to the left. Two symbols representing his brothers were placed below him, while two symbols representing his brothers-in-law, his sister, and her husband were included as well.

SOCIOMETRIC ANALYSIS

My sociometric analysis of the social atoms completed by Linda and Alan during their therapy considered the number of symbols, size, distance, gender, balance, and relationships, as well as missing symbols, and the roles the symbols represented.

Social Atom One Analysis: Linda

The first social atom was completed by the couple as an assessment of their functioning, as shown in Figures 10–1 and 10–2. Linda's diagram included nine symbols, an average number, with a somewhat equal distribution of males and females. All of these were family members. From the style of her matrix, her use of size

Figure 10–9: Alan's Third Social Atom

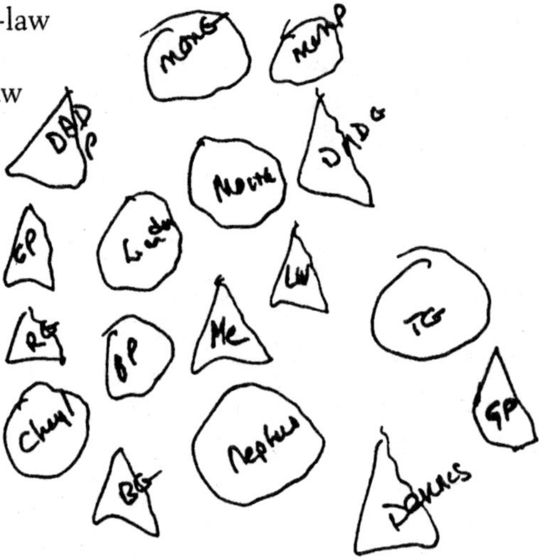

Mom G. = Mother-in-law

Dad G. = Father-in-law

Mom P. = Mother

Dad P. = Father

B.P. = Brother

C.P. = Sister

T.G. = Sister-in-law

Dennis = Brother

R.G. = Brother-in-law

B.G. = Brother-in-law

D.P. = Brother

Cheryl = Sister-in-law

G.P. = Sister-in-law

L.W. = Son

Moira = Daughter

Linda = Wife

Nephews = Brother's children

Figure 10–10:
Linda's Perception of Alan's Third Social Atom

Moira = Daughter

Lee = Son

His Mom = Mother-in-law

His Dad = Father-in-law

My Mom = Mother

My Dad = Father

Him = Husband

Me = Wife

Ron = Brother-in-law

Bill = Brother-in-law

Barry = Brother

Jerry = Friend

Dennis = Brother

Cheryl = Sister-in-law

and space, one could conclude that she was expansive in her style of relating to the world. In exploring the meaning of Linda's underlining of her own symbol, questions related to her own identity confusion and her uncertain position in relationships with others would need to be expanded in therapy.

Linda appeared to have completely differentiated herself from others. There were no overlapping symbols, which is typical of someone with undifferentiated boundaries. The symbols used to indicate her children were equal in size to that of her husband. Several hypotheses were raised with regard to the meaning of the equal size of these symbols. Were her children as important to her as her husband? Did the size of these symbols support the weighted position of parent she was experiencing in the marriage? Did the larger size of her symbol indicate the visibility she experienced in the family? All the symbols drawn were equidistant from her own, with the exception of her in-laws, which were clearly drawn further away. How close did she really feel to others?

During the treatment process, the completed social atoms were reintroduced and these questions explored. The exploration of the atoms with the couple prompted Linda to explain to Alan how important she considered her role as the parent, and her desire to provide the children with the nurturing she had never received from her parents. She and Alan then discussed the neglect she had experienced as a child and her strong desire not to repeat that cycle. During one session, Linda further explained that she felt like the more visible parent, the parent the children always sought out. Alan was unaware of the importance Linda placed on her role as parent or how overburdened and unsupported she felt by him in the role. These conflicts as well as others needed to be explored more fully and resolved.

Social Atom One Analysis: Alan

The size of the symbols in Alan's first diagram, with the exception of Linda, Moira, and Lee, which were larger, were all equal. Was his immediate family more important to him than his extended family? In the diagram, Alan placed his two children closest to him. Was Alan feeling closer to his children than to his wife? The lack of space in this diagram suggests that Alan may have felt overwhelmed and too responsible for others. The placement of his son suggests a possible wedge he may have experienced between Linda and himself. Perhaps Alan felt overpowered by Linda, which may explain his choice of a larger symbol to represent her. These hypotheses were explored with Alan in treatment to gain more information, to increase his awareness, and to offer an avenue of discussion between Linda and Alan.

The completed social atom was reintroduced to Alan during a couples therapy session where he explained that, in fact, his immediate family was important to him and that at times he did feel closer to his children than to his wife. During therapy sessions, Alan would occasionally complain that Linda expected too much of him as a mate and parent, and placed the children before him. These complaints brought out the dynamics between Alan, Linda, and their children for further review and change.

In Alan's first social atom diagram (Figure 10–2), he had a somewhat cluttered grouping of figures, many symbols in close proximity. Was this lack of space indicative of his feeling overwhelmed and too responsible for others? His style of organization suggested possible constriction and a persuasive attention to details. Several figures were equal in size to his own figure. This was a very different social atom from his wife's. One example among many was that Linda used a larger symbol for herself, while Alan's symbols were more or less of equal size. Each mate viewed the world very differently. How did this affect their personalities?

Social Atom Two Analysis: Linda

Midway in treatment the couple was asked to complete a second set of social atoms, to review any changes in each partner's self-assessment. Linda's had eight symbols, all closely drawn

(Figure 10–3). Was she feeling closer to others? The symbols of her children and husband were equal in size to hers. Was she experiencing more balance in her life?

In her second social atom, Linda chose to represent herself and Alan much closer than in the first diagram, actually touching. The figure she used to represent herself was also more clearly outlined than the earlier one. Was Linda gaining a better sense of herself than she had at the beginning of therapy? This idea needed to be explored in therapy.

Her son Lee was deeply overlined, as was the figure for the therapist, indicated by a J. Some confusion about the importance and significance of these two relationships in her life is perhaps indicated by the overemphasized drawings. In addition to the therapist in this second social atom diagram, the symbol for a friend was also included. The placement of these two configurations was explored with Linda, both for information and to create further awareness. Any symbols that were missing or had been added from the first diagram were also addressed, such as the fact that her in-laws were not in the second configuration, although they had been included in the first.

Showing Linda both the first social atom and the second one, three months later, and asking her what she noticed as different would open the discussion. During the follow-up session to the second social atom diagramming Linda and Alan had completed, the couple were shown their first and second social atom diagrams and asked to share their perceptions of the differences they saw in the diagrams.

Added marks to any symbol in the atom are known to have a significance, although often unconscious. It would be important at this point to unintrusively question Linda about her son, such as "How is Lee doing? How is your relationship with your son? Do you have any concerns about him?" Once that relationship's information is explored, I would move to questions related to myself, since the other symbol also has additional demarcations. Additionally, in a session following the second social atom diagramming, Linda was asked to describe my significance in her social atom. She explained the dependent feelings she was experiencing as she became more aware of her need to have me, as the therapist, show her how to communicate effectively with her husband. Aware of this, I could in a lighter, joking tone respond to Linda by saying, "I would imagine that it's not always easy to speak to me about our relationship, but please feel free to talk to me or ask me about anything that relates to our relationship," or ask each mate, "How would you describe our relationship on a scale of one to ten, ten being great and one being terrible?" A statement such as this, or a similar one based on the therapist's style and relationship with the couple, could offer the opportunity for further exploration of each mate's social sphere and perceptions.

Social Atom Two Analysis: Alan

When a client is experiencing depression, the symbols depicting others are often drawn larger than the symbol used to represent the self. Alan continually reiterated that he suffered from depression. The clutter of symbols within a small space that existed in Alan's first diagram is considerably lessened in the second diagram (Figures 10–2 and 10–5). There were now five symbols in the drawing instead of twelve. Is Alan feeling better about himself? Did he believe the couples therapy was helping? These questions and others similar to the ones below were addressed in therapy.

Alan was asked if he thought the decrease in the number of symbols in his social atom had any significance. He explained that he felt more comfortable telling Linda during the sessions how pressured he felt. He said she didn't seem to understand the pressure of her demands, but he felt the sessions provided a safe environment in which to express his feelings to her.

In Alan's second diagram (Figure 10–5), his symbols were somewhat more equal in size and proximity. It became obvious that the distance he may have been experiencing from others needed to be addressed in therapy. The symbols for his children were drawn the closest to his own symbol. Was he feeling closer to his children? Did the equality of size have some meaning for him? When these questions were addressed in therapy, Alan explained that he did feel closer to his children than he did to Linda, although he wished he could feel closest to her. He indicated that he found her demands stressful and therefore maintained distance from her. Alan also explained that he considered everyone equal, that he found no one person more significant than another to him. He believed Linda would like to be more important to him, but that was not how he viewed his world. Alan appeared to have a clearer sense of himself in this later diagram than he had in the previous one. The symbol for himself was finely drawn and closer to his wife than in the original diagram (Figure 10–2), indicating that he was experiencing a clearer understanding and sense of himself, as well as a closer relationship to his wife. In addition, the symbols did not appear to be shakily drawn, indicating he was experiencing a greater sense of stability.

Social Atom Three Analysis: Linda

In the third social atom completed by Linda (see Figure 10–7), she represented herself at least three times larger than any other symbol. Was she feeling the need to consider herself more? Was she feeling more expansive? These hypotheses were addressed by, "You drew the symbol for yourself somewhat larger. Does that have any significance for you?"

In this diagram, there were no other symbols touching her own. Was she feeling distant from others? This was another hypothesis to be addressed in therapy to elicit Linda's perception of how she was using space in the diagram and her life, thereby generating a discussion to create awareness as well as information. For example, her diagram could be viewed again and a statement directed to her, "Linda, take a look at your diagram. Do you believe it depicts how you see yourself in your environment?" Then I might add, "Do you have any reactions when you look at it?" That could be followed by a question such as, "Does the size and distance you created in the diagram depict accurately the amount of space and significance you give yourself in the world?" Adding on, "What do you make of it?" This could be followed with a discussion suggesting to both Linda and Alan that they take a look at how differently they depict themselves in this world.

The symbol used to represent Alan was placed directly above her own. Did this have any meaning to her? Was she feeling that he added something to her life that was representative of this placement? These were additional hypothetical questions to be addressed with Linda in sessions. Moreover, she now represented herself in a clearer and more proportioned manner than in the earlier diagram. This may have indicated a further clarification of identity and an added indication she was experiencing improvement in her self-worth. She was asked whether she felt more enriched. Linda explained that she understood Alan better and how to manage her reactions to his responses to her requests. She added that learning how to discipline herself when interacting with Alan made her feel more assured about herself. Linda had a tendency to address Alan in an abrupt, confrontive style. Actually, she had no idea that her questions were confrontive; she knew only that Alan's responses showed annoyance or frustration, and that was obviously not her intention. She noted again that observing how I, as the therapist, interacted with them during the sessions offered her alternate ways of discussing her needs with Alan.

The emphasis she had placed on her son and the therapist in the earlier diagram (Figure 10–3) had been eliminated. Her children, however, continued to be represented by figures equal in size to that of her husband. Their importance in her life remained highly emphasized. It is not unusual to find a person who is not in touch with her own childhood pain or trauma to project unconscious personal needs for protection, concern, or significance onto her children. Having repressed or detached from her own pain, she transposes her feelings onto another as "projection identification." There is limited differentiation for Linda between herself and her children, especially her son. Role playing will in time assist her in further developing the needed differentiation of boundaries. Her boundaries will become more defined as she enacts role presentations with the various auxiliaries in her life. Linda's boundary difficulties become dynamically represented in her role reversal with Alan. At times during sessions, when she was asked to take his role, she would switch back to being herself without knowing it. This occurrence offered me an opportunity to point out what took place and discuss how she does that in various situations, pointing out to her that her boundary switch, if you will, does not function properly. Her lines of connection with others are loose, which causes her at times to assume what others are experiencing, to project herself into their being.

Linda's last social atom showed a possible decline in functioning. The symbols for others were more distant from her than in the previous diagram. During the therapeutic process of couples psychotherapy each partner was asked to draw another social atom to see if there was any change in their functioning. Linda appeared to be feeling more withdrawn since the news of Alan's impending job loss. Her social atom showed the distancing (symbols for auxiliaries were drawn further from her than previously). The hypothesis drawn about Linda's preoccupation with Alan's absorption in reading was a projection of her own depression. The sense of defeat and helplessness that she had disowned and was consciously unaware of was projected onto her husband. Linda is somewhat symbiotic in nature; her boundaries with Alan do not remain clear (as has been observed in role reversals) so Alan's self-absorption would leave her feeling abandoned and unable to feel whole, since she believes she needs him to make her universe whole.

Had Alan's job loss, his depression, and self-absorption left her feeling anxious? Was Linda totally financially dependent on Alan? And if this were true, was she feeling helpless? Was she feeling inadequate? Questions for further sessions.

In the sessions that followed, Linda revealed how helpless she felt. In fact she was extremely anxious about their financial situation and felt overwhelmed about what to do. Since she hadn't worked for ten years, she was worried at the thought of having to reenter the job market and manage a household with young children. These issues needed to be explored so that each partner could present his or her views and come to some decisions.

Social Atom Three Analysis: Alan

In the third and last social atom completed by Alan (Figure 10–9) his functioning appeared to have declined. There were seventeen configurations. The symbols that represented himself, Linda, his son, and daughter were shakily drawn in comparison with the first two diagrams, especially his own. The overall diagram was more cluttered in appearance than earlier atom drawings. His daughter and son were placed in a manner that separated him from his wife, who was more clearly drawn and larger than the symbol representing himself. Did Alan now have a better sense of Linda's identity than he did of his own? Was he still experiencing stress from Linda's demands to perform certain roles? Was Alan feeling unsupported in the world and was this why his symbols were shakily drawn? He had the symbols for his children on one side of himself and the symbol representing Linda placed on his other side—all at some distance from him. Was he, in fact, feeling distant and withdrawn from others?

Alan's diagram was not as distinctive or clearly drawn as the previous two diagrams he had completed. Moreover, the size of his symbol was no larger than those of his wife and children. Did this indicate his limited sense of worth and regard for himself? You will recall that in the time interval between his second and third diagrams, Alan was terminated as vice president of a prominent banking firm due to the depressed economy. Because he was unable to find a similar position, he had joined a consulting firm at a much lower salary. Obviously, this change had shaken Alan's sense of financial security and his self-esteem. This instability was exemplified in the diagram.

During the session when we discussed the last social atoms, I asked Alan if the shakiness of his symbols had any significance. He revealed that he had gone through bouts of depression before, but losing his job had been overwhelming. He felt a strong loss. He had no idea how he was going to support his family. This intervention offered the couple an opportunity to explore Alan's employment situation and some of his professional loss in further depth.

These projective diagrams provided other information about each mate's perception of the other. For example, was each partner able to role reverse with his or her mate and approximate a diagram similar to that of their spouse? The skill of role reversal required to approximate their mate's position is extremely valuable for couples and demonstrates the ability of a mate to have empathy for the other. When these atoms were completed by Alan and Linda, I found that each partner's projective drawing resembled the one he or she had done of their own social atom. The use of size and space on each projective atom was unlike their mate's. Neither partner was able to complete a successful projective diagram of the other's social matrix in the middle or at the end of treatment—they were unable to accurately role reverse. The apparent differences in the way they saw each other, the delusions and fantasies they harbored about how the other related to the world needed to be explored and clarified in therapy.

ROLE ASSESSMENT

The AMP role assessment sequence is a two-part diagnostic procedure. The pre-test and post-test include a self-assessment and a projective assessment by each partner of his or her mate's role assessment of the relationship. This gives a clearer view of each partner's role choices in the relationship—the roles they spend the most time in, the roles that are prominent in the relationship, the roles they value, and the roles that are considered an important part of the relationship by each partner.

The role choices and the status of the choices in a relationship reveal the components and structure of a relationship, the relationship's personality, the complementary, conflicting, and inhibited aspects of the partnership.

A role assessment from each mate is requested when they entered therapy (Table 10–1). Each partner is asked to make a list of roles he or she considers prominent in their relationship; roles in which they spend the most time. They are then asked to rank each role's prominence in ascending order starting with the most prominent role at the bottom of the list. The term *prominent* was used to indicate those roles in which each partner spent the most time.

Additionally, a compiled list of roles important to their relationship, the roles they most value, is requested. A ranking of their importance in ascending order was then completed. The roles chosen by each are listed in ascending order, number 1 being the first choice in each category, as shown below.

Table 10–1: Role Assessment One

Self-Perception (Linda)		Partner's Perception (Linda)	
Prominent	Important*	Prominent	Important*
4-Parent	4-Friend	6-Patient	6-Dependent
3-Wife	3-Lover	5-Lover	5-Child
2-Patient	2-Parent	4-Friend	4-Parent
1-Child	1-Wife	3-Dependent	3-Friend
		2-Parent	2-Lover
		1-Wife	1-Wife

Self-Perception (Alan)		Partner's Perception (Alan)	
Prominent	Important*	Prominent	Important*
4-Husband	4-Lover	4-Husband	4-Lover
3-Supporter	3-Parent	3-Supporter	3-Parent
2-Parent	2-Supporter	2-Parent	2-Supporter
1-Doctor	1-Husband	1-Doctor	1-Husband

*Important is considered a "wished-for" category.

Role Analysis One: Linda

In her role analysis (Table 10–1), Linda indicated that she valued the parent role significantly, giving it a 2 in importance; however, she rated it as 4 in prominence, meaning that she spent the least time in that role. She spent a little time in the wife role, rating it as 3 in prominence. But she valued that role the most, rating it as 1 in importance.

In this role assessment, she chose the role of child as most prominent, for it was the role most used in their relationship at the time. Yet she had no ranking of this role as of any importance in relating to Alan. Although Linda viewed herself as spending a lot of time in the patient role, rating it as a 2 in prominence, she did not see it as a valued role—it was not listed as an important role.

Did Linda want to be more independent, to be treated like a woman and feel like a wife, but lacked the skills? She often felt like a child in the relationship, as indicated by the rating she gave that role in the assessment. Did she want to change this role position? Would she like to try some other roles and styles of relating? Answers to these questions would be sought in therapy. For example, the role assessment, in a follow-up session, was addressed with the following statement to Linda, "You rate child as a role you spend considerable time in, especially in relationship to Alan. But you didn't rate it as a valued role. Is that because you would like to eliminate it from the role repertoire you have in your relationship with Alan? Would you like to explore some role training with Alan to find other roles you both may find more enjoyable or rewarding?"

These questions were explored in a follow-up session, and as Linda viewed her assessment, she agreed that she would like to feel more like a woman in relation to Alan and not so much like a child. She shared those feelings with him. In response, Alan described the womanly traits she did have and other traits in women that he admired. Although the couple indicated they would like further role training in this area, there were other needs, such as managing their fears and conflicts over Alan's job loss, that took precedence. However, they had their role assessments as reminders and these role positions could be further explored at a later date.

In Alan's perceived assessment of role choices (Table 10–2), he indicated he thought Linda would choose wife as the most prominent role, followed by parent, dependent, friend, lover, and patient.

Role Analysis One: Alan

In Alan's first role analysis, he chose husband as most important, followed by supporter, partner, and finally lover. He indicated that he spent the least time in the husband role, rating it as number 4 in importance, but noted he valued that role the most, rating it as 1 in prominence. Did Alan enjoy the husband role? Would he like to explore other traits of that role that he and Linda could enjoy?

Alan chose as the most prominent role, the role in which he spent the most time in the relationship, that of doctor, followed by parent, supporter, and husband. He indicated that he spent most of his time in the role of a doctor; however, it was not a role he valued. Did Alan really want to relinquish this role but felt Linda needed his help? As was already indicated, Linda was an adolescent-onset diabetic who neglected her illness, as did her parents. When Alan met her, he was concerned about her health and started overseeing the stabilization of her diabetes. He had

assumed responsibility for giving her the daily insulin and check-
ing her sugar level. Was the burnout Alan was experiencing from
the duties he had assumed as designated doctor of Linda's care
affecting their relationship? Had the burden and conflict intensified Linda's diabetic comas and her reliance on Alan? These
questions needed to and would be explored in the process of
treatment so the couple could explore their role options.

Table 10−2: Role Assessment Two

Self-Perception (Linda)		Partner's Perception (Linda)	
Prominent	Important*	Prominent	Important*
6-Wife	5-Companion	6-Patient	6-Dependent
5-Mother	4-Lover	5-Lover	5-Child
4-Doctor	3-Partner	4-Friend	4-Parènt
3-Companion	2-Friend	3-Dependent	3-Friend
2-Partner	1-Wife	2-Parent	2-Lover
1-Friend		1-Wife	1-Wife

Self-Perception (Alan)		Partner's Perception (Alan)	
Prominent	Important*	Prominent	Important*
6-Parent	6-Child	4-Husband	5-Companion
5-Lover	5-Parent	3-Friend	4-Lover
4-Friend	4-Supporter	2-Companion	3-Partner
3-Doctor	3-Friend	1-Partner	2-Friend
2-Husband	2-Lover		1-Husband
1-Supporter	1-Husband		

*Important is considered a "wished-for" category.

Role Analysis Two: Linda

In her second role assessment (Table 10−2), Linda chose friend,
followed by partner, companion, doctor, mother, and wife as the

roles where she spent most of her time. As the more valued and important roles, she chose wife, followed by lover, friend, partner, and companion. Despite the fact that she perceived wife as her most valued role at that time, it was the role she spent the least time in.

Linda's perception of Alan's most valued roles was that of husband, followed by friend, partner, lover, and companion. She thought he would choose partner as the most prominent and utilized role in the relationship, followed by companion, friend, and husband.

Role Analysis Two: Alan

In Table 10–2, Alan points out that he thinks that Linda's choice as the most important and valued role choices in their relationship to be that of wife, followed by lover, friend, parent, child, and dependent. Moreover, he also wished Linda would choose the role of wife as the most prominent, followed by parent, dependent, friend, lover, and patient.

He chose the role of husband for himself as the most important and valued role, followed by lover, friend, supporter, parent, and child. And although Alan gave lover as his second most valued role in his marriage, he revealed that he actually spent little time in that role. He chose the role of supporter as his most prominent and utilized role, followed by husband, doctor, friend, lover, and parent.

Interestingly, the roles of friend and companion entered into the role configuration in this present assessment (Table 10–2), although they had not been chosen as roles in the earlier assessments.

In the foregoing role assessment of this couple's marriage, the conflicts and challenges that they have experienced are exposed. The level, style of intimacy, and need of each mate in this partnership is decidedly different. Linda's desire to have Alan as a friend was not reciprocated by Alan, for he had chosen the more traditional role of wife for her. Their difference in style is exemplified by the difference of this choice. Alan's was a much more formal presentation of roles than Linda's, which is truly exemplified in their difference in style, dress, and role choices. This lack of complementary role needs has to be addressed in the ongoing therapy so that both mates can be aware of their differences and move toward change or acceptance.

In discussion Alan actually told Linda that he did not want to be her friend, and Linda was able to express her feelings of rejection in response to his statement. To add clarity to the interaction, I first doubled Alan's desire for a more traditional style of marriage, and then Linda's desire for a more intimate relationship was also doubled. The differences they were experiencing in their roles were further defined, clarified, and redefined.

ROLE ASSESSMENT REVIEW

Believing that each individual's personality is a composite of his or her roles and that role conflict, role inhibition, or the hunger for a new role affect a couple's interpersonal relationship, a decision was made to have each partner in this couples therapy complete an assessment of the roles each performed and spent the most time in, and also in relationship to each other. The couple was also asked to rank the roles they valued most in their relationship. Comparing the roles they valued most with those that they spent the most time in would indicate where conflicts lay and where needed role changes should be explored. For example, Alan and Linda needed to learn how they both contributed to the doctor/patient relationship, with Alan needing to learn how to relinquish that role.

The role of doctor in Table 10–1 was experienced by Alan as a burden. Linda's ongoing diabetic comas and her reliance on him for help with insulin injections and psychological nurturing, which she had never received from her own parents, had placed him in a role he found very debilitating. He was expected to watch her diet, yet she wanted to be independent and treated more like a woman instead of a sick child. But this was the role she chose, and this was the role he responded to. Role training was needed to assist them in achieving satisfaction in more mature and satisfying role choices. Several sessions were therefore spent exploring the early doctor/patient roles they had assumed in their relationship. The process of doubling each partner's feelings and thoughts was continued, and then alternative styles of relating and complementary role choices were explored.

The doctor/patient role the couple had emphasized at the beginning of treatment, and in the early social atom diagrams, was almost eliminated in the last diagram (see Table 10–2). Linda's role of patient had now receded to sixth place in Alan's perception. She now took care of her own insulin and diet and had sufficiently matured to eliminate the child role from her own diagram.

Burnout exists in any role that was rated as one or two in prominence but was the least rated in value. Time minus value equals burnout. For example, Alan had not written the role of doctor in his role diagram as a role he valued in his relationship. Therefore, as the therapist, I formed a hypothesis to be checked out with the client. In this case, Alan mentioned that he had experienced burnout in the role of doctor, burnout meaning he had no more energy, tele, to give to the role. With this in mind, work had to be directed toward changing that role pattern as soon as possible to eliminate any more stress on the relationship.

Both partners indicated that the roles they chose as most valued were not the roles they spent the most time in. Their last assessment indicated that they still had not chosen each other reciprocally for the same roles, nor were they even aware of the roles in which their mates were experiencing burnout. The procedure of having each mate rate his or her perception of the other's role choices was instituted to see if they could reverse roles. This procedure was also repeated at intervals, as were the role assessments, to see if there was any improvement in either partner's ability to step into the other shoes.

Linda's assessment of Alan's roles shows how unaware she was of the importance he gave to his role as a supporter and parent. He rated that role as number one, the role in which he was spending the most time. In Linda's list of prominent roles that she thought Alan would choose, she saw him as companion and friend, but he never saw himself in that light.

Although Linda had a smaller role repertoire than Alan, the roles she had chosen were more complementary to a marital relationship, for example, the roles of wife, friend, partner, lover, and companion. She, therefore, experienced less stress or role burnout in the relationship. Alan's repertoire of roles in the relationship were less intimate than Linda had wanted. The roles of supporter, husband, and doctor, ranked as the three most prominent roles in the relationship, carry a strong responsibility, and all fall into a caretaking category. They also include a role that was not identified as valued or important to him, the role of doctor. Linda's list of prominent roles, in contrast, includes roles that she also valued. The sequence and priority of roles were different in both lists, which shows her struggle to find a balance; however, she is not experiencing the stress that Alan is in performing a role for which he finds no value.

Linda and Alan continued to have difficulty reversing roles. The roles each partner listed in the diagram as the perceived roles, those roles they believed their partner to be experiencing, were inaccurate. It could be seen from the diagram that both Linda and Alan assumed that their partners were experiencing the same roles in the relationship as they were. This indicates their difficulty in reversing roles with each other, their inability to step into the shoes of the other. Linda and Alan needed to learn how to devote more time to the roles they valued in this relationship. They were spending time in the roles they did not consider to be important. Role retraining was needed.

CHAPTER

11

$\backsim$

Did the Therapy Help?

The use of AMP, with its tools and techniques of role reversal, mirroring, and doubling, provides new methods in which the couple can free themselves from their constant arguing.

The couple presented in the previous chapter, Alan and Linda, did make progress. They eliminated the most conflictual doctor/ patient roles from their marital relationship repertoire during the course of treatment. However, the discrepancy evident in role choices, such as Alan choosing the female partner as confidante in the "wished-for" role category, and Linda wanting Alan as a companion, created conflict in their relationship. Linda wanted Alan to share in her choice of activities, while Alan still preferred that she choose others, and that led to Linda's feelings of rejection.

Alan chose Linda as someone to confide in and someone from whom he might receive support. One can imagine his feelings when she suggested that he go to colleagues for such support. These areas, although not creating as much role conflict as the doctor/patient roles had, needed to be further explored and negotiated.

Alan's inability to cope with the loss of his job and his subsequent feelings of inadequacy in the community might have been more severe if he had not been in treatment. Although I hoped that couples psychotherapy would offer him improved ways of coping, the loss for him was profound. The intrapsychic issues raised for him stemming from his own abusive background were perhaps too overwhelming. Linda and Alan were in such need of validation and approval that they found themselves unable to take responsibility for their own perceptions and behaviors. They operated in a state of blindness, alienated from parts of themselves. They disowned and projected their unacceptable disowned roles and attitudes onto their partner, typical in a dysfunctional marriage. Participation in an effective marital therapy required this couple to develop a sense of trust—trust in the process of therapy, trust in me as their therapist, trust in themselves, and a willingness to experience the vulnerability of disclosure. They had developed a trust in me early on; however, a trust in themselves and each other was difficult to obtain given their sense of alienation.

Alan did not have a clue as to how he appeared to others, especially his wife. He had little perception of how other roles he had developed in interactions with others operated. He found the video therapy sessions somewhat alarming, for he had no sense of the impact he had on others. Viewing the videos of the marital sessions for him was like seeing a movie about someone else. Linda also found viewing herself in the videos amazingly difficult. She said that although Alan was recognizable, she disliked seeing herself. She could not get over how she looked and acted. The entrenched blindness and disowned aspects of themselves were portrayed before them; their alienation from themselves and from their relationship was challenged. Although trust in the process of therapy and in my skills had been attained earlier, they now began to gain trust in themselves and to expand their observing ego roles. This self-confrontation had long-lasting effects on their subsequent behavior. I encouraged them to review the videos at home, stop them where they wanted to make changes, role play those changes, including doubling and role reversal, and come in the following week to discuss their successes. They began to work together, using the video of their interactions and the AMP tools to help.

Linda and Alan came to realize that their marriage had not been made in heaven. They learned that since they had never had an accurate and complete sense of themselves their choice of a partner may not have been the best. Their tele (chemistry with each other) was deficient, not conducive to intimacy. Neither one was able to accurately double (speak each other's inner thoughts and feelings) without my assistance at first. They came to realize that many of the ghosts from their relationship with their parents or their parents' relationships had invaded their own relationship, and were permanent, if not welcome, guests in their home. They became aware that if they wanted the relationship to succeed they would have to put forth effort to change the role patterns they had assumed. The action methods they learned of doubling and role reversal aided them in communicating. Alan and Linda became able to assess a disruptive communication pattern, stop, and attempt to double each other. They learned to take "time out" to assess their own behaviors. Alan and Linda agreed that although they would constantly have to make an effort to keep the relationship stable, they were willing to do so. The sense of achievement they received from overcoming obstacles seems to have given them the satisfaction they needed to continue. They found that the AMP skills they learned in marital therapy offered them conjoint ways of parenting each other when necessary. Gradually they assumed suitable role patterns in their relationship. This couple had more difficulty than most because of the extreme alienation they had developed; however, their desire to improve and work on the relationship fortified their ability to improve their marriage.

Alan would have benefited from individual treatment during his job loss crisis. However, when that intervention was suggested, it was refused. Had they not been in therapy during this crisis, would Linda have had an understanding of how Alan was feeling or any idea of how to respond to his needs? Perhaps not. The couples therapy sessions offered him an opportunity to discuss his loss and the stress of his job search in a safe forum. Linda sat and listened to his struggle in the sessions and gained greater insight and empathy. She gained empathy as she began to be able to reverse roles with her husband. Alan learned how to communicate his struggle instead of withdrawing from it. The crisis might have had an even more profound effect on their marriage had they not been in treatment.

The role assessments were useful, for they revealed at a glance the role stressors and the changes desired by each partner. They also highlighted the complementary roles that each partner had chosen in the relationship, their role conflicts, and those areas where their role choices needed to be renegotiated and new role training encouraged.

HOW THEY FELT

In their last videotaped session, Linda and Alan agreed that they found the course of treatment helpful. Alan found that they now argued much less than they did prior to therapy. He also added that he had become more comfortable speaking up on his own behalf. Moreover, they were beginning to solve some disagreements on their own. He discovered they no longer needed to wait until their next therapy session to resolve a conflict.

Linda also saw improvements in their relationship. She said she was now able to tell him what she was feeling without getting upset and yelling. Watching how I spoke with her partner during the sessions gave her new ideas of what to say and how to say it. Her approach became less combative and more assertive. It was a whole new world.

The use of the AMP soliloquy technique (shown on pages 83–126) illuminated how I identified with Linda and how I pursued more of a therapeutic push to have her expand her awareness and interpersonal skills. As a therapist, I had a strong sense of the increased despair that Alan had been experiencing in response to the loss of his position as vice president of a bank, and approached him more cautiously. Occasionally, my countertransferential responses to his loss kept me from addressing and expanding his thoughts and feelings. My fear of his repressed rage and anger may have kept me from encouraging him to stretch and improve his performance. I avoided exposing his anger and subsequently could not articulate for Linda the feelings or thoughts she had been experiencing in response to his contained rage. However, she did experience a more visible catharsis in the sessions and, therefore, improved at what appeared to be a more significant rate. Did she improve more than Alan intrapsychically? Only time would tell. Also, since Linda did not experience the emotional crisis of job loss during the sequence of therapy, she was not in that state of grief Alan experienced, and she could therefore devote herself to improving her interpersonal skills.

DOUBLING TECHNIQUE EVALUATION

The Action Modality Psychotherapy doubling procedure used in the couples sessions was significantly useful and helped to expand each partner's ability to communicate. Using the process increased each partner's ability to expand and concretize feelings and thoughts and then relate them to the other. The procedure also aided each partner in developing listening skills. As statements made by either partner were embellished and clarified by the therapist, each mate came to further understand and empathize with the other's position. Both partners also received role training as they observed how I doubled the mate. This demonstrated to each the importance of validating the other and summarizing what was communicated by the other.

For example, following Alan's job loss and career crisis, he became withdrawn during several of the sessions. The doubling of his feelings of helplessness and loss enabled him to get in touch with just how overwhelmed he was really truly feeling. Once concretized, these thoughts and feelings no longer remained intrapsychic in nature, and he was then able to further share and expand with his partner what he was really going through. Prior to this interception he was bound intrapsychically; he was autotelic, incapable of interpersonal communication. There were weeks when he prefaced each session by saying he had told Linda that she would have to wait until they had a therapy session to talk about the job situation because he felt unable to articulate his feelings and thoughts to her. As the therapy continued following the job crisis, he reestablished himself and again began to communicate on issues with his mate outside of the sessions. As a result, the couple's relationship became more balanced.

OUTSIDE INFLUENCES

In treating couples, or indeed in any therapy situation, it is important to remember that things happen in the broader world that may influence the therapeutic process. Coping with the loss of job and role status in the community may have been more severe had they not been in treatment. The job loss for Alan was so devastating that I believe he required individual treatment. It was suggested but refused. In many ways, the issues and needs that grew out of his job loss were inappropriate for couples treatment.

OTHER INFLUENCES

Obviously things happen in a therapy session that may affect performance. For example, toward the end of their therapy I confronted the couple, saying it was my perception that over the last few months they had given me the responsibility for their relationship and had not been working on improving their marriage outside of the sessions. Although it was a thought-out intervention on my part, this procedure could have had a strong impact on the couple's functioning.

FOLLOW-UP (1995)

This couple was followed up three years after the completion of their marital therapy. At that time several changes had taken place. Alan had taken a position as a consultant in a finance company. He was putting in long hours, making less money, but finding the work much more enjoyable. He was also taking an antidepressant. When asked if it helped, he said, "Well, I guess. I'm getting done what I have to."

Linda had taken a job and was enjoying being out of the house and meeting people. Both the children had been seen for brief counseling. When asked if they found that AMP had provided them with skills to aid their relationship, both partners agreed that it had. They added that it was something they had to keep up with, practice, and stay mindful of, which at times they put off.

Alan suggested that a six-month follow-up session would have been helpful. When invited to come in for a refresher session, both partners agreed. They would like to do that again in the near future and added that the only reason they had not called for an appointment was because of finances. Their economic status since Alan's job loss in banking had changed considerably. They were now living on a much more restricted budget and appeared to have some shame related to this change in economic status, although with prompting they agreed to consider a follow-up appointment in the near future. Follow-up phone contact will be maintained.

CONCLUSIONS

In summing up the discussion of Alan's and Linda's relationship, the partnership appeared to improve over the course of treatment and the relationship became more balanced. Their ability to communicate and empathize with each other did improve. Alan became more proficient at showing his difficulties and frailties and less frightened of taking and giving comfort and reassurance to Linda. In the past, rather than show the frustration he was experiencing in his relationship to her, he acted out his frustration in an extramarital relationship. Now he was able to explore and express his feelings of inadequacy and conflict in response to her requests. And Linda, over the course of treatment, had increased her ability to understand and empathize with her partner's thoughts and feelings. She came to understand that he was not rejecting her as a person when he disagreed with her opinion.

Action Modality Psychotherapy is a valuable tool for work with couples. The AMP approach to doubling and near doubling for each mate helps the individual and the partner expand and deepen their awareness and expression of their feelings. Doubling does assist each mate in developing empathy for their partner. The mirroring at specific times, such as when either partner asks how he or she is perceived by the other, is effective. Gaining a perspective on how a behavior is being perceived by their partners does assist each mate in redefining and adjusting their behaviors to suit the intention of their individual needs.

Role reversal training does assist both mates in clarifying their partner's point of view. Stepping into their partner's shoes also helps them gain empathy for their partner. The use of video recording the therapeutic process with couples using the AMP approach (a mirroring technique) is helpful. A couple is ready for this step when they start asking how they are perceived. However, when and how to introduce video reruns of a session to a couple remains questionable—timing is key.

The AMP role assessments method is a valuable tool. It provides concrete, observable ways of identifying a couple's role conflicts. This method can be useful to therapists who use other types of psychotherapeutic modalities as well.

The elements of psychodrama and sociometry, introduced and developed by J. L. Moreno at the turn of the century, and further developed into the therapeutic entity of AMP, are a viable treatment modality for use with couples.

Epilogue

The therapist guides the journey.
Establishing the soul-connection
    therapist-client is the first step.

Moving forth with a guide,
    not a knower, is truly a release from the
    authority of socialization to the autonomy of
    brother or sisterhood.

The therapist guides the journey.
Faith that there is a universality,
    a vibration that transcends capturing one's place of release.
    The sense of splitting—reestablishes the disconnection.
    The bond of birthing—recreates a source of oneness.
    The god of being. The I-thou creation.

The therapist guides the journey.
Requires openness to change,
    openness meaning release of control.
Perhaps gently in the beginning until openness becomes an
    exciting, valuable, treasured opportunity.
A view of life as a continually opening, awakening,
not a journey of death—closure.

The therapist guides the journey.
A journey that is a continual rebirthing process.
Life as an unfoldment.

A rebirthing of the soul until such time that it reaches
    expansion and moves from body to universality—
    spirit—known as death on this plain of action.

APPENDIX

I

જ

Characteristics of a Conscious Relationship

1. Realize your love relationship has a hidden purpose: the healing of childhood wounds.
2. Create a more accurate image of your partner.
3. Take responsibility for communicating your needs and desires to your partner.
4. Learn to value your partner's needs and wishes as highly as you value your own.
5. Embrace the dark side of your personality.
6. Learn new techniques to satisfy your basic needs and desires.
7. Search within yourself for the strength and abilities you are lacking.
8. Become more aware of your drive to be loved, united, and whole with the universe.
9. Accept the difficulty of creating a good marriage.
10. Read Hendrix, *Getting the Love You Want* (1988).

II

࿔

AMP Questionnaire for Couples Contemplating Therapy

AMP PART I:

Please indicate your rating of the following statements:

  1 = Always
  2 = Most of the time
  3 = Some of the time
  4 = On occasion
  5 = Seldom
  6 = Never

  1. We communicate effectively.
  2. Our sexual relationship is fulfilling.
  3. Our affection responses are fulfilling.
  4. We manage conflict effectively.
  5. We divide chores.
  6. The quality of the future is promising.

7. We manage money effectively.
8. I am committed to the relationship.
9. My partner is committed to the relationship.
10. We support each other's careers.
11. The way we make decisions is effective.
12. I feel my partner and I fight.
13. My partner threatens physical violence.
14. I threaten divorce or separation.
15. Have you ever abused your mate?
16. Has your mate ever abused you?
17. My relationship with my partner's relatives is fulfilling.
18. My partner's relationship with my relatives is fulfilling.

AMP PART II:

List three role changes you would like to see in your partner:

List three role changes you believe your partner would like to see in you:

List three issues or situations that trigger conflict with your partner:

List three topics that you believe need to be discussed with your partner:

List three topics you think your partner believes need to be discussed:

Identify challenges in your relationship:

AMP PART III:

Using a rating scale of one through five, one being the highest, make two lists. In the first, list your goals in the relationship. In the second, list your perception of your partner's goals in the relationship:

1. Improve a satisfying relationship.
2. Improve a relationship that offers little satisfaction.
3. Decide whether to continue the relationship.
4. Resolve conflicting feelings so relationship can be ended peacefully.

Identify significant previous relationships:
How many?

Age at outset:	Relationship 2	Relationship 3
Age at ending:	Relationship 2	Relationship 3
Reason for ending:	Relationship 2	Relationship 3

Number of children from each relationship:
How does the current relationship compare with the others:
(use a rating scale, one being the most satisfying)

What additional information needs to be considered:

III

⌘

The AMP Renewal Boutique for Couples

A technique used to tap into a couple's intimacy is the AMP Renewal Boutique, a communication technique introduced to gather information, coupled with a guided imagery exercise to better acquaint couples with their childhood wounds. The couple is asked to close their eyes, listen to some soothing music, and try to remember their early childhood environment. As the vision begins to sharpen, they are asked to see themselves as very young children wandering around the house searching for one of their parents. The therapist then tells them that they are suddenly endowed with magic powers: they can see the positive and negative traits of this parent with crystal clarity. They are asked to imagine themselves telling that parent what they always wanted from them and never got. They are then asked to move along and encounter any other person who has had a profound influence on their formative years. After gathering all the information about these key people, they are slowly brought back to reality and asked to take time to reflect and write down the key information they have received. When this is completed, the couple is asked to share what they've learned and listen attentively to each other, making no effort to assess or analyze remarks presented. Further understanding of this approach is explained in Chapter 3.

References

Abrams, J. C., and Kaslow, F. W. (1976). Learning disabilities and family dynamics. *Journal of Clinical Child Psychology* 5:35–40.

Ackerman, N. W. (1958). *The Psychodynamics of Family Life*. New York: Basic Books.

——— (1966a). *Treating the Troubled Family*. New York: Basic Books.

——— (1966b). Family psychotherapy: Theory and practice. *American Journal of Psychiatry* 20:405–414.

——— (1970). *Family Therapy in Transition*. Boston: Basic Books.

——— (1982). The family approach to marital disorders in the strength of family therapy. In *Selected Papers by Ackerman*, ed. D. Bloch and R. Simon. New York: Brunner/Mazel.

Adler, G. (1948). *Studies in Analytical Psychology*. New York: Norton.

——— (1953). The relationship of mental status to incidence and recovery from mental illness. *Social Forces* 32:185–194.

——— (1958). Social role and personality. In *The Psychodynamics of Family Life*, p. 235. New York: Basic Books.

——— (1961). *The Living Symbol*. London: Rutledge & Kegan Paul.

——— (1964). Superiority and social intention. In *Social Intention*, ed. H. L. Ansbacher and R. Ansbacher. Boston, MA: Northeastern University Press.

——— (1966a). The psychology of power. *Journal of Individual Psychology* 22:166–188.

———— (1966b). *Treating the Troubled Family*. New York: Basic Books.

———— (1980). *What Life Should Mean to You*. London: George Allen American Publishing.

———— (1983). *The Practice And Theory Of Individual Psychology*. Allendale: Rowan and Allenheld.

Alexander, F. (1968). *An empirical study on the differentiated influence of self concepts of the professional behavior of marriage counselors*. Unpublished dissertation, University of Southern California.

Alice, A. (1960). *Healthy and Disturbed Reasons For Having An Extramarital Affair*. New York: Grune & Stratton.

Allon, S. E. (1978). *Exploration Of The Social Atom*. Unpublished manuscript.

Allport, G. (1959). Discussion of the first lecture. Transference, counter-transference and tele. Their relation to group research and group psychotherapy. In *Psychodrama Vol. 2*, ed. J. L. Moreno, p. 314. New York: Beacon Press.

Arzin, N., Naster, B., and Jones, R. (1973). Reciprocity in counseling: a rapid learning based procedure for marital counseling. *Journal of Behavior Research and Therapy* 6:365–382.

Atwater, L. (1979). Getting involved in women's transition to first extramarital sex. *Alternative Life Styles* 2:41–68.

———— (1982). *The Extramarital Connection*. New York: Irvington Press.

Bates, C. N., and Brodsky, A. M. (1988). *Sex in the Therapy Hour: A Case of Professional Incest*. New York: Guilford.

Bateson, G. (1979). *Mind and Nature: A Necessary Unity*. New York: Bantam.

Berger, M. (1978). *Video Techniques In Psychodrama Training and Treatment*. New York: Brunner/Mazel.

Bion, W. R. (1959). *Second Thoughts*. New York: Basic Books.

Bohannon, P. (1970). *Divorce and After*. Garden City, NY: Doubleday.

Boszormenyi-Nagy, I., and Framo, J. (1967). *Intensive Family Therapy*. New York: Harper and Row.

Boszormenyi-Nagy, I., and Spark, G. M. (1973). *Invisible Loyalties*. New York: Harper and Row.

Bowen, O. H. (1954). *An investigation of the therapeutic relationship in client-oriented therapy.* Unpublished doctoral dissertation. Chicago: University of Chicago.

——— (1971–1972). Toward the differentiation of self in one's family of origin. In *Georgetown Family Symposium.* Washington, DC: Georgetown University Medical Center.

——— (1976). Theory in practice of psychiatry. In P. Guerin (ed.), *Family Therapy.* New York: Gardner.

——— (1978). *Family Therapy In Clinical Practice.* Northvale, NJ: Jason Aronson.

Bowlby, J. (1973). Attachment and loss. In *Separation, Anxiety and Anger, Vol. 2.* pp. 9–52. New York: Basic Books.

Brown, E. M. (1991). *Patterns of Infidelity and Their Treatment.* New York: Brunner/Mazel.

Buchanan, D. (1980). The central concern model: a framework for structuring. *Journal of Group Psychotherapy, Psychodrama And Sociometry* 33:47–62.

Burgess, E. W., and Locke, M. W. (1945). *Husbands and Wives: The Family From Institution to Companionship.* New York: American Books.

Burgess, R. L. (1981). Relationships in the marriage. In *Personal Relationships,* ed. W. Duck and R. Gilmore, pp. 251–255. New York: Academic.

Chasin, R., Roth, S., and Bograd, M. (1989). Action methods in systemic therapy: dramatizing ideal future and reformed pasts with couples. *Family Process* 28(1):121–136.

Compernolle, T. (1981). J. L. Moreno: an unrecognized pioneer of family therapy. *Family Process* 20:331–335.

Cutler, B., and Dyer, W. (1973). Initial adjustment process in young married couples. In *Love, Marriage, Family: A Developmental Approach,* ed. M. Lasswell and T. Lasswell, pp. 475–489. Glenview, NY: Scott Foresman and Company.

Dicks, H. V. (1967). *Marital Tensions.* London: Routledge.

Duvall, E. (1967). *Family Development.* Philadelphia: Lippincott.

Ellis, A. (1949). A study of human love relationships. *Journal of Genetic Psychology* 75:61–71.

Erhardt, A., and Money, J. (1980). *Gender Identity, Man and Woman, Boy and Girl*. New York: New York University Press.

Erickson, M. H. (1950). Indirect hypnotic therapy of a bed wetting couple. *Journal of Clinical and Experiential Hypnosis* 12:171–174.

Fairbairn, W. R. D. (1954). *An Object Relations Therapy of Personality*. New York: Basic Books.

Framo, J. L. (1981). The integration of marital therapy with sessions with families of origin. In *Handbook Of Family Therapy*, ed. A. S. Gurman and D. P. Knisken, pp. 133–158. New York: Brunner/Mazel.

——— (1990). Integrated families of origin into couples therapy. In *One Couple/Four Realities: Multiple Perspectives On Couples Therapy*, ed. R. Chasin, H. Grunebaum and M. Herzig, pp. 49–82. New York: Guilford.

Frank, L. K. (1961). *The Conduct of Sex*. New York: Grove.

Freud, S. (1900). *The Interpretation of Dreams*. London: Hogarth Press.

——— (1905). *Three Essays on the Theory of Sexuality*. New York: Basic Books.

Fromm, E. (1956). *The Art Of Loving*. New York: Harper and Row.

Gibran, K. (1927). *The Prophet*. New York: Knopf.

Giovacchini, P. L. (1965). Treatment of marital disharmonies: The classical approach. *International Journal of Group Psychotherapy* 18:185–202.

Glick, R. D., Clarkin, J. F., and Kessler, D. R. (1987a). The content of family evaluation. In *Marital and Family Therapy*, 3rd ed., pp. 128–139. New York: Grune & Stratton.

——— (1987b). Family treatment. In *Marital and Family Therapy*, 3rd ed., pp. 167–187. New York: Grune & Stratton.

——— (1987c). Formulating and understanding family problem areas. In *Marital and Family Therapy*, 3rd ed., pp. 140–157. New York: Grune & Stratton.

——— (1987d). The functional family. In *Marital and Family Therapy*, 3rd ed., pp. 45–110. New York: Grune & Stratton.

Grunebaum, H. (1976). Some thoughts on love, sex, and commitment. *Journal of Sex and Marital Therapy* 2:277–283.

Guerin, P. J., Fay, L. F., Burden, S. L., and Kautto, J. G. (1987). *The Evaluation and Treatment of Marital Conflict.* New York: Basic Books.

Gullick, E. L. (1983). The marital relationship: adapting an old model to contemporary needs. In *Treatment Interventions in Human Sexuality*, ed. C. C. Nadelson and D. B. Marcotte, pp. 377–420. New York: Plenum.

Gurman, A. S. (1978). Contemporary marital therapies: analysis of psychoanalytic behavioral and systems theory approaches. In *Marriage and Marital Therapy*, ed. T. J. Paolino and B. S. McGrady, pp. 595–608. New York: Brunner/Mazel.

Gurman, A. S., and Kniskern, D. P. (1981). Family therapy research: knowing and intent. In *Handbook Of Family Therapy*, ed. A. S. Gurman and D. P. Kniskern, pp. 742–776. New York: Brunner/Mazel.

Hale, A. E. (1981). The role diagram expanded. In *Conducting Clinical Sociometric Explorations: A Manual for Sociometrists and Psychodramatists.* Roanoke, VA: A. E. Hale.

Haley, J. (1963). *Strategy of Psychotherapy.* New York: Grune & Stratton.
——— (1976). *Uncommon Therapy: The Psychiatric Techniques of Milton H. Erickson, M.D.* New York: Norton.

Hart, J. (1974). An outline of basic postulates of sociometry. *Journal of Psychotherapy, Sociometry And Psychodrama* 33:63–69.

Hendricks, G., and Hendricks, K. (1990). *Conscious Loving.* New York: Bantam Books.

Hendrix, H. (1980). *Getting the Love You Want.* New York: Harper and Row.

Hill, C. T., Rubin, Z., and Deplau, L. A. (1976). Breakups before marriage: the end of affairs. In *Divorce and Separation*, ed. G. Levinger and O. Moles. New York: Basic Books.

Hollander, S. E. (1974). Social atom: an alternative to imprisonment. *Journal of Group Psychotherapy* 27:172–183.

———— (1978). *An Introduction to Sociogram Construction.* Denver: Lion Press.

———— (1983). Comparative family systems. *Journal of Group Psychotherapy, Psychodrama and Sociometry* 36(1):1–12.

Hudgins, K., and Kiesler, D. J. (1984). *Instructional Manual for Doubling in Individual Therapy.* Richmond: Virginia Commonwealth University.

Jackson, D. D. (1965). Family—marital quid pro quo. *Archives of General Psychiatry* 12:589–694.

————, ed. (1970). *Communication, Families and Marriage.* Palo Alto, CA: Science and Behavior Books.

Jackson, D. D., and Lederer, W. L. (1973). Sex in marriage. In *Love, Marriage, Family: A Developmental Approach*, ed. M. Lasswell and T. Lasswell, pp. 296–301. Glenview, NY: Scott Foresman.

Jackson, D. D., Risken, J., and Satir, V. (1961). A method of analysis of a family interview. *Archives of General Psychiatry* 5:332–339.

Jacobson, N., et al. (1982). Reactivity to positive and negative behaviors in distress and undistressed married couples. *Journal of Consulting Clinical Psychology* 50:706–714.

———— (1985). A component analysis of behavioral marital therapy—one year follow-up. *Behavior Research and Therapy* 23:549–555.

Jacobson, N., and Margolin, G. (1979). *Marital Therapy: Strategies Based on Several Learning and Behavior Exchange Principles.* New York: Brunner/Mazel.

Jennings, H. H. (1943). *Leadership and Isolation: A Study of Personality in Interpersonal Relations.* New York: Longmens.

Johnson, J. R., and Campbell, L. E. (1988). *Impasses of Divorce in the Dynamics and Resolution of Family Conflicts.* New York: Free Press.

Karpel, M. (1980). Family secrets: I. Conceptual and ethical issues in the relationship context; II. Ethical and practical issues in therapeutic management. *Family Process* 19:295–306.

Katz, S. J., and Liu, A. E. (1991). *The Codependency Conspiracy. How to Break the Recovery Habit and Take Charge of Your Life.* New York: Warner Books.

Kautto, J. G., Leo, F. F., and Guerin, P. J. (1987). *The Evaluation and Treatment of Marital Conflict.* New York: Basic Books.

Kinsey, C., et al. (1953). *Sexual Behavior in the Human Male.* Philadelphia: W. B. Saunders.

Klein, M. (1969, 1973). Mourning and its relation to mania and depression states. In *The Interpretation of Death,* ed. H. Ruitenbeck, pp. 114–125. Northvale, NJ: Jason Aronson.

Kniskern, D. P., and Gurman, A. S. (1978). Research on marital family therapy: Progress, perspective and prospect. In *Handbook of Psychotherapy and Behavior Change,* S. L. Garfield and A. E. Bergin (eds.) (2nd ed). New York: Wiley.

———— (1981). *Handbook of Family Therapy.* New York: Brunner/Mazel.

Lawson, A. (1988). Personal correspondence in Brown, E. M., *Patterns of Infidelity and Their Treatment.* New York: Brunner/Mazel.

LeFrancois, G. R. (1984). Life stage choices. In *The Life Span,* pp. 416–419. Belmont, CA: Wadsworth.

Lerner, H. G. (1989). *The Dance of Intimacy: A Woman's Guide to Courageous Acts of Change in Key Relationships.* New York: Harper and Row.

Lewis, H. B. (1979). Gender identity: primary narcissism for primary process. *Bulletin of the Menninger Clinic* 43(2):145–160.

Linton, R. (1936). *The Study of Man.* New York: Appleton Century Press.

Marineau, R. F. (1989). *Jacob Levy Moreno 1889–1974.* New York: Routledge.

Markman, M. (1979). Application of a behavioral model of marriage in predicting relationship satisfaction of couples planning marriage. *Journal of Consulting and Clinical Psychology* 47:743–749.

Masters, W. H., and Johnson, V. E. (1963). *Human Sexuality.* Boston: Little, Brown.

———— (1976). *The Pleasure Bond: A New Look at Sexuality and Commitment.* New York: Bantam.

Mittlemann, B. (1948). The concurrent analysis of couples. *Psychoanalytic Quarterly* 17:182–197.

Minuchin, S., and Fishman, H. C. *Family Therapy Techniques*. Cambridge, MA: Harvard University Press.

Moreno, J. L. (1914). *Einladung Zu Einer Begegnung*. Vienna: Anzergruber Verlag.

—— (1915). *An Invitation To An Encounter*. New York: Beacon House.

—— (1916). *Das Testament des Schweigens (Philosophy of Silence)*. Vienna: Anzengruber Verlag.

—— (1923). Intermediate (in situ) sociometry. In *Psychodrama II*, pp. 124–163. New York: Beacon House.

—— (1934). *Who Shall Survive*. New York: Beacon House.

—— (1937a). Psychology of interpersonal relations. *Journal of Sociometry* 1:3–5.

—— (1937b). Intermediate (in situ) treatment of a marital triangle. *Sociatry* 1:124–163. Reprinted in J. L. Moreno, *Psychodrama, Volume 3*. New York: Beacon House.

—— (1939). Psychodramatic shock therapy: a sociometric approach to the problem of mental disorders. *Sociometry*, Vol. 1, No. 1, p. 5.

—— (1940). The psychodramatic treatment of marriage problems. *Journal of Sociometry* 3:1–23.

—— (1945). Role tests and role diagrams of children. *Journal of Sociometry* Vol. 3, p. 10.

—— (1946a). Situation tests. *Sociometry*, Vol. IX, No. 2, p. 3.

—— (1946b). *Psychodrama: Volume One*. New York: Beacon House.

—— (1947). *The Theatre of Spontaneity*. New York: Beacon House.

—— (1952). Psychodramatic production techniques. *Journal of Group Psychotherapy, Psychodrama and Sociometry* 4:273–303.

—— (1953). *Who Shall Survive? A New Approach to the Problem of Human Interrelations*. Washington, DC: Nervous and Mental Disease Publishing Company.

—— (1956). *Sociometry and the Science of Man*. New York: Beacon House.

—— (1960). *The Sociometry Reader*. New York: Free Press.

—— (1966). The creativity theory of personality, spontaneity, creativity, and human potentials. *New York University Bulletin. Arts and Science* 164.

——— (1969). Psychodramatic rules, techniques and adjunctive methods. *Journal of Group Psychotherapy* 22:213–219.

——— (1975). Mental catharsis and the psychodrama. *Journal of Group Psychodrama and Group Psychotherapy* 26(3–4):5–32.

——— (1977). Role testing for a marriage. In *Psychodrama, Volume 1*, pp. 153–176. New York: Beacon House.

——— (1987). Psychodrama, role theory and the concept of social atom. In *The Evolution of Psychotherapy*, ed. J. K. Zeis, pp. 170–179. New York: Brunner/Mazel.

Moreno, J. L., and Moreno, Z. T. (1938). Interpersonal therapy and psychotherapy of interpersonal relationships. *Sociometry II* 4:25–31.

——— (1941). *Words of the Father*. New York: Beacon House.

——— (1969a). *Psychodrama, Volume 3*. New York: Beacon House.

——— (1969b). Psychodrama of a marriage: first session. In *Psychodrama, Volume 3*, 2nd ed., pp. 16–17. New York: Beacon House.

——— (1975). *Psychodrama, Volume 2*. New York: Beacon House.

Moustakas, C. (1972). *Loneliness And Love*. Englewood Cliffs, NJ: Prentice-Hall.

Murstein, B. (1974). *Love, Sex and Marriage Through The Ages*. New York: Springer.

Nadelson, C., et al. (1983). Conjoint marital psychotherapy treatment and techniques. *Journal of Diseases of the Nervous System* 3:253–259.

Napier, A. Y. (1978). The rejection-intrusion pattern: A central dynamic. *Journal of Marriage and Family Counseling* 4:4–5.

National Center for Health Statistics (1986). Washington, DC: U.S. Government Printing Office.

Norton, A. J., and Glick, P. C. (1979). Marital instability in America: past, present and future. In *Divorce and Separation: Context, Causes and Consequences*, ed. G. Levinger and O. C. Moles, pp. 3–37. Orlando, FL: Basic Books.

Olsen, D. H., Portner, J., and Bell, R. (1952). Marriage and sex life. In

Sexual Adjustment in Marriage, pp. 38–59. New York: Henry Holt.

——— (1983). Faces II items. In *Marriage and Family Assessment: A Sourcebook for Family Therapy*, ed. E. E. Felsinger, pp. 250–279. Beverly Hills: Sage Publications.

Papp, P. (1983). *The Process of Change*. New York: Guilford.

Paul, N. L. and Paul, B. B. A. (1975). *Marital Puzzle*. New York: Norton.

Penn, P. (1982). Circular questioning. *Family Process* 21:265–280.

Perez, P. (1975). Personal interaction for married couples. *Acta Psiquiatriay Psicologica de America*, Latina: 2.

Pollis, C. (1969). Dating involvement and patterns of idealization: a test of Waller's hypothesis. *Journal of Marriage and Family Therapy*, November, p. 770.

Prochasker, J. O., and Prochasker, R. S. (1978). Toward the development of an interpersonal approach. In *Focus of Brief Therapy*, ed. S. Budner, pp. 415–457. New York: Guilford.

Rappaport, R. (1964). Normal crisis, family structures, and mental health. *Family Process* 2:68–80.

Roger, C. R. (1975). An unappreciated way of being. *Counseling Psychologist* 5:2–10.

Rollin, E., and Feldman, H. (1973). Marital satisfaction over the family life cycle. In *Love, Marriage, Family: A Developmental Approach*, ed. M. Laswell and T. Laswell, pp. 321–324. Glenview, NY: Scott Foresman.

Rubin, Z., et al. (1979). Breakups before marriage: the end of 103 affairs. In *Divorce and Separation: Context, Causes and Consequences*, ed. G. Levinger and O. Moles, pp. 54–83. New York: Basic Books.

Sager, C. J. (1974). Sexual dysfunctions and marital therapy. In *The New Sex Therapy*, ed. H. S. Kaplan. New York: Brunner/Mazel.

——— (1974–1976). *Marriage Contracts and Couples Therapy*. New York: Brunner/Mazel.

——— (1976). The role of sex therapy in marital therapy. *American Journal of Psychiatry* 133:55–550.

Sager, C. (1981). Couples therapy and marriage contracts. In *Marital and Family Therapy* (3rd ed.), ed. I. D. Glick, J. F. Clarkin, and D. R. Kessler. Orlando, FL: Grune & Stratton.

Scarf, M. (1987). *Intimate Partners*. New York: Random House.

Schnarch, D. M. (1991). *Constructing the Sexual Crucible*. New York: Norton.

Schulz, D. A. (1981). *Marriage, The Family and Personal Fulfillment*. Englewood: Prentice-Hall.

Sherman, R. and Friedman, N. (1986). *Handbook of Structural Techniques in Marriage: Family Therapy*. New York: Norton.

Siroka, R. (1987, 1988, 1989, 1990, 1991, 1992, 1993). *Individual Supervision*. New York: pp. 107, No. 2.

Skynner, A. C. (1976). *Systems of Family and Marital Psychotherapy*. New York: Brunner/Mazel.

Solomon, L., and Grunnebaum, H. (1982). Stages in Social Development. *Hillside Journal of Clinical Psychiatry* 4:95–126.

Solomon, M. F. (1981). *Narcissism and Intimacy*. New York: Norton.

Stanton, M. (1981). An integrated structural-strategic approach of family therapy. *Journal of Marital and Family Therapy* 7:427–429.

Stein, M. B., and Callahan, M. L. (1982). The use of psychodrama in individual psychotherapy. *Journal of Group Psychotherapy, Psychodrama and Sociometry* 35:1–29.

Stone, J. (1990). Who is most likely to remarry. In *The Extramarital Affair*, pp. 13–57. New York: Free Press.

Strean, H. S. (1980). *The Extramarital Affair*. New York: Free Press.

Stuart, R. B. (1976). An operant interpersonal psychotherapy for couples. In *Treating Relationships*, ed. D. H. L. Olsen, pp. 327–351. Lake Hills, NY: Alpine.

Stuart, R. B., and Stuart, B. J. (1985). *Second Marriage*. New York: Norton.

Stuckert, R. P. (1973). Role perception and marital satisfaction: a configuration approach. In *Love, Marriage, Family: A Developmental Approach*, ed. Lasswell and Lasswell, pp. 377–381. Glenview, NY: Scott Foresman.

Taylor, J. (1977). *Investigative Studies of the Social Atom*. Unpublished manuscript. St. Elizabeth Hospital requirement for residency.

Tharp, R. G. (1963). Psychological patterning in marriage. *Journal of Marriage and Family Living* 60:97–117.

Toeman, Z. (1948). The double situation in psychodrama psychiatry. *Journal of Group and Intergroup Therapy* 1(4):436–559.

Watzlawick, P. (1978). *What is Change*. New York: Basic Books.

———, et al. (1967). *Pragmatics of Human Communications*. New York: Norton.

——— (1974). *Change: Principles of Problem Formation and Problem Resolution*. New York: Norton.

Weakland, J. H., et al. (1974). Brief therapy: focused problem resolution. *Family Therapy* 13:41–168.

Weingarten, K. (1980). *What is Systemic Therapy?* Unpublished manuscript, Family Institute of Cambridge, MA.

Weiss, R. L. (1975). Contract: cognition and change. A behavioral approach to marriage therapy. *Counseling Psychologist* 5:15–26.

Whitaker, D. A. (1975). Family therapist looks at marital therapy. In *Couples in Conflict: New Directions in Marital Therapy*, ed. A. S. Gurman and D. Rice. Northvale, NJ: Jason Aronson.

Williams, A. *The Passionate Technique*. New York: Tavistock/Routledge.

Yalom, I. D. (1975). *The Theory and Practice of Group Psychotherapy*, 2nd ed. New York: Basic Books.

Index